Happiness Studies

"In a masterful lesson, a master teacher integrates literature, philosophy, psychology, economics, and other disciplines to elucidate what happiness is and how to pursue it. In symphonic harmony, conceptual elegance and empirical evidence blend to emit new scholarly tunes. This book will lift your spirits, encourage you to look after your physical well-being, enrich your intellect, and move you to get closer to your loved ones and to your emotions. Tal Ben-Shahar has succeeded in creating a synoptic framework for studying and practicing happiness and well-being."

—Isaac Prilleltensky, co-author, with Ora Prilleltensky, of *How People Matter: Why it Affects Health, Happiness, Love, Work, and Society*

Tal Ben-Shahar

Happiness Studies

An Introduction

Tal Ben-Shahar
Attention: Raphael Sagalyn
c/o ICM Partners
New York, NY, USA

ISBN 978-3-030-64868-8   ISBN 978-3-030-64869-5   (eBook)
https://doi.org/10.1007/978-3-030-64869-5

This Palgrave Macmillan imprint is published by the registered company Springer Nature Switzerland AG.
The registered company address is: Gewerbestrasse 11, 6330 Cham, Switzerland

To Marva Collins (1936–2015)
You continue to inspire me

Fig. 1 Author with Marva Collins. (Photo Credit: CJ Lonoff)

ACKNOWLEDGMENTS

I would like to begin by thanking Megan McDonough and Maria Sirois. Together, we embarked on the journey of Wholebeing, and together we uncovered the magic of SPIRE. Their words, and even more so their spirits, are present throughout the book.

The Happiness Studies Academy is my dream come true. It would not be a reality without my dear partner and friend Yuval Kutz, who masterfully integrates between vision and execution, the abstract and the concrete. Andrea Ding, Naomi Eckhardt, Shelly Kelman, Rachel Lavie, Greg Li, Sahar Maimony, Tami Muller, Or Porat, Liad Ramot and Arlen Solodkin are fellow pioneers who, with remarkable humbleness and competence, dedicate themselves to our students and to a happier world.

Udi Moses has been by my side from the very first and precarious steps of this journey—helping, challenging, encouraging and carrying. I stand on his shoulders. Rouben Madikians, more than anyone I know, embodies the essence of servant leadership, providing me and numerous others with the strength and courage to forge our path. I am grateful every single day for CJ Lonoff's professionalism and generosity—for her hawkish editorial eyes and her heart that is as big as the ocean.

I am grateful to Craig Collins, whose mind-prints and fingerprints are pervasive throughout the book. He elevates my writing, with his incisive intelligence and genuine gentleness. Jennifer Kurdyla lavishly sprinkled her passion and brilliance throughout the book, helping me say more with less. To Sandra Happi-Tasha, my deepest gratitude for your wisdom and insights—I am because we are.

Phil Getz from Palgrave Macmillan is everything a writer could ask for in a publisher and editor—brilliant, razor-sharp and caring. I so appreciate the number of hours he spent dissecting the ideas and then patiently helping me stitch them back together again. Amy Invernizzi's meticulous attention to details made the whole so much better. Stuart Halpern is the ultimate giver; without his fervent generosity this book would not have found its publishing home. To the two reviewers, who remain anonymous, a big thank-you for your insightful and helpful comments.

Being represented by the Sagalyn Literary Agency has been a great gift, from the time I started writing. Rafe Sagalyn, much more than my agent, is a dear and trusted friend. Brandon Coward and Tia Ikemoto are quiet leaders who seamlessly bring together caring and professionalism.

The number one predictor of happiness is the quality of our intimate relationships. My beloved family, on Friday nights and throughout my life, provides me with an abundance of life's ultimate currency.

I'm dedicating this book to the memory of Marva Collins, my role model and inspiration. It was when I first heard of her work as an educator that I resolved to become a teacher; and it was when I first met her that I realized that if we want to be in the light, we have to help those around us shine.

Contents

LIST OF FIGURES

PART I

Introducing Happiness Studies

CHAPTER 1

Why Happiness Studies?

One has to spend so many years in learning how to be happy.
—Mary Anne Evans[1]

July, 2015. A transatlantic flight, somewhere between London and New York City. The monotonous hum of the plane; the slow-moving clouds; the tranquil expanse of water, miles below, that somehow seems within reach—all these soothe me into a state of calm repose. My mind is clear, open. And in this meditative state a question strikes me: How is it that there are fields of study dedicated to literature, psychology, physics, business, history, and dozens of other subjects, and yet none dedicated to the study of happiness?

Yes, there is positive psychology, which is the field that I had immersed myself in for almost two decades, but that's just the psychology of happiness. What about a discipline, or rather an interdisciplinary field, that takes what psychologists have to say about happiness and combines it with what philosophers, economists, theologians, artists, biologists and others all have to say about the good life?

The lack of an interdisciplinary program of happiness studies is particularly puzzling considering the almost universal agreement on the centrality of happiness in our lives. We want to be happy, and we want those we care

T. Ben-Shahar, *Happiness Studies*,
https://doi.org/10.1007/978-3-030-64869-5_1

about to be happy. Aristotle, more than 2000 years ago, argued that happiness is the "most desirable of all things … something final and self-sufficient, and is the end of action."[2] Even before the wise Greek, the wise King Solomon expressed similar sentiments, claiming that the highest life goal is to "rejoice, and to do good."[3] In *The Alchemy of Happiness*, Al-Ghazali, an eleventh-century Persian theologian, claimed that the ultimate prize of self-knowledge and devotion to God is happiness.[4]

The United States Declaration of Independence, written by Thomas Jefferson a year into the American Revolutionary War, declared it a "self-evident" truth that the pursuit of happiness was an unalienable human right. Echoing this sentiment, Helen Keller wrote that "most of us regard happiness as the proper end of all earthly enterprise. The will to be happy animates alike the philosopher, the prince and the chimney-sweep. No matter how dull, or how mean, or how wise a man is, he feels that happiness is his indisputable right."[5]

This focus on happiness is not restricted to Western thinkers. The Chandogya Upanishad, a Hindu text that is among the world's oldest religious scriptures, declares that happiness is to be found not in the limited, trivial things of the world, but in the infinite.[6] Confucius, the teacher and philosopher of China's Spring and Autumn period (the fifth century BCE), invokes joy and pleasure in the two opening lines of the *Analects*.[7] In his book *The Art of Happiness*, based on 2500 years of Buddhist teachings, the current Dalai Lama proclaims that, "Whether one believes in religion or not, whether one believes in this religion or that religion, the very purpose of our life is happiness, the very motion of our life is toward happiness."[8]

The idea common to these and other thinkers is that happiness is the highest on the hierarchy of goals, the end toward which all other ends lead. Wealth or wisdom, accolades or accomplishments, are subordinate and secondary to happiness; whether our desires are material or social, they are merely *means* toward what I've come to call life's *ultimate currency*.[9] Any other currency—be it in the form of money or prestige—only has value if it can yield, or be exchanged for, happiness.

If happiness is indeed the highest end, or even if it is merely one of many goals that matters to us, then dedicating effort to understanding and exploring it is a worthy pursuit. And yet, in 2015 there was not a single institution of higher learning anywhere in the world that offered a degree in happiness studies. There were a handful of positive psychology degree programs and some dedicated to the philosophy of happiness, and then there were programs that took a very specific and narrow approach to cultivating wellbeing. But in contrast to programs in economics, for instance, no academic program in happiness focused on both micro happiness (individuals and relationships) as well as macro happiness (organizations and nations). No academic program in happiness embarked on an interdisciplinary approach, analogous to a rigorous medical school curriculum, in which different fields of inquiry merged to shed light on a particular subject.

One of the reasons for the conspicuous absence of happiness studies has been the difficulty of coming to a consensus on what this field ought to look like. What is happiness? What are the core principles that define the structure of the field? What topics and ideas make up its substance? Should any subject that includes the word "happiness" be part of the field, no matter the context in which the word is used or its implied meaning? Or should any word associated with happiness—such as "joy," "flourishing," "fun," "purpose" or "pleasure"—be a criterion for inclusion? Which topics related to the good life—wholly or in part, directly or indirectly—should find their way into a happiness studies curriculum?

These are just some of the questions I will address in this book, in an attempt to create a coherent, interdisciplinary field of life's ultimate currency. I must point out, though, that the blueprint I am proposing in the following pages—the structure and the substance of the field—is a conversation starter, not a decree. I am inviting you to actively engage in an urgently important dialogue surrounding the good life—a dialogue that ought to be a part of this fascinating field and can itself be a source of much happiness.

*   *   *

Ever since my transatlantic flight in 2015, I have been tirelessly advocating for the study of happiness, in academia and elsewhere. The question I am often asked, both by those who support my idea and by those who reject it, is: *Why?* Why spend time and effort reading extensively about happiness, or getting a certificate in happiness studies, or going even further and pursuing a degree in the field?

My answer to this question is exactly the answer I would give to justify studying anything—but in this case, the answer is far more concrete and immediate, far less abstract and removed. Here's what I mean: If you asked an MBA candidate *why* she chose to pursue a business degree, she might say, "So that I can become a better businesswoman." If you probed further and asked her *why* she would want to become a better businesswoman, she could respond, "So that I can make more money." And if you continued with another *why* or two, she would ultimately arrive at, "So that I (or those I care about) can be happier."

You could follow the same interrogation protocol with a student of law or astrophysics or education or anthropology, and get the same results. Within one *why* or a few *whys*, the answer will eventually arrive at increasing the person's own or others' happiness, or at some related concept, such as feeling good or finding meaning. As the ultimate currency—the highest on the hierarchy of goals, the end toward which all other goals lead— happiness is the justification for investing time and effort in any pursuit. In the words of British philosopher David Hume, considered one of the fathers of modern Western philosophy: "The great end of all human industry is the attainment of happiness. For this were arts invented, sciences cultivated, laws ordained, and societies modeled."[10]

Why study happiness, then? For the same reason you would study any other field or discipline, namely to become happier and to help those you care about become happier. And if it seems obvious to people why they would study business or engineering or sociology, then, it should be even clearer to them why they would study happiness. There are fewer degrees of separation—fewer *whys*—between the study of happiness and life's highest end than there are between any other course of study and that same end.

Now that we're clearer about the *why*, we're ready to move on to the *what*. In the next chapter I will provide a definition for happiness, and in Chaps. 3 and 4, I'll break down this definition into its elements and principles.

One reason for introducing the elements and principles is, as I will discuss in Chap. 5, to present a coherent structure for an academic class, a degree course or a book on happiness studies. A second, no less important, reason for introducing the components and principles is to help you better understand, pursue, and attain happiness. Throughout this book, for these two reasons, I freely and frequently shift between offering academic analysis and providing self-help advice, between the abstract and the concrete, between theory and practice, between understanding life's ultimate currency and living happily ever after.

Notes

1. Eliot, G. and Cross, J. W. (ed.). (1887). *George Eliot's Life: As Related in Her Letters and Journals*. W. Blackwood and Sons.
2. Aristotle. (1954). *The Nicomachean Ethics* (D. Ross, Trans.). Oxford University Press.
3. Ecclesiastes 3:12, *King James Bible*.
4. Al-Ghazzali, A. B. (2017). *The Alchemy of Happiness* (C. Field, Trans.). Martino Fine Books.
5. Keller, H. (1903). *Optimism: An Essay*. T.Y. Crowell.
6. *The Upanishads* (Swami Paramananda, Trans.). CreateSpace Independent Publishing.
7. Confucius. (1998). *The Analects* (D. C. Lau, Trans.). Penguin Classics.
8. Dalai Lama. (2009). *The Art of Happiness: A Handbook for Living*. Riverhead Books.
9. Ben-Shahar, T. (2007). *Happier: Learn the Secrets to Daily Joy and Lasting Fulfillment*. McGraw-Hill Education.
10. Hume, D. (1985). *Essays: Moral, Political, and Literary*. Liberty Fund Inc.

CHAPTER 2

Happiness as Wholebeing

To me the only satisfactory definition of happiness is wholeness.
—Helen Keller[1]

So what is happiness? There have been many answers to this question, ranging from the absence of suffering to the experience of pleasure, from living a life of meaning to fulfilling one's potential, from cultivating our body to saving our soul, from serving others to actualizing the self, and the list goes on. Here's a small sample of the countless attempts to define happiness.

Psychologist Sonja Lyubomirsky defines happiness as "the experience of joy, contentment, or positive well-being, combined with a sense that one's life is good, meaningful, and worthwhile."[2] Denis Waitley, a motivational speaker and consultant, offers an alternative definition: "Happiness is the spiritual experience of living every minute with love, grace and gratitude."[3] To former track star and cardiologist George Sheehan "Happiness is different from pleasure. Happiness has something to do with struggling and enduring and accomplishing."[4] Then there is the very serious definition by Stoic Roman philosopher Seneca—"Human happiness is founded upon wisdom and virtue"[5]—and the very adorable definition by Charles Schulz, creator of the *Peanuts* comic strip—"Happiness is a warm puppy."

© The Author(s), under exclusive license to Springer Nature
Switzerland AG 2021
T. Ben-Shahar, *Happiness Studies*,
https://doi.org/10.1007/978-3-030-64869-5_2

Given the plethora of definitions, most people don't believe they need a formal definition of happiness, and instead approach it as they approach the concept of beauty. While they may not be able to define beauty, their argument goes, they know it when they see it; similarly, while they may not be able to define happiness, they know it when they experience it. I would argue that to leave the concept of happiness undefined—to settle for a murky and unclear approximation of what the good life entails and exacts of us—is to compromise on our ability to understand, pursue and attain it.

Two decades ago, when I first started to write about life's ultimate currency, I defined happiness as "the overall experience of meaning and pleasure."[6] This definition was my attempt to encompass both the impermanence of the pleasurable emotions that come with happiness, and the deeper sense of life's purpose and meaning. It also hints at how the temporary and enduring aspects of happiness are interdependent and mutually reinforce each other.

Over the years, based on the growing body of research within Positive Psychology and based on my exploration of other disciplines—from philosophy to anthropology, from theology to neuroscience—my thinking evolved beyond understanding happiness as the integration of meaning and pleasure. Today, the definition I find most useful as a student and teacher of happiness draws on the words of Helen Keller who more than a century ago wrote: "To me the only satisfactory definition of happiness is wholeness." Drawing on Keller's words, I define happiness as "the experience of wholeperson wellbeing." To further simplify the definition, melding the compound words *wholeperson* and *wellbeing*, one might say that happiness is "the experience of *Wholebeing*." In the next chapter I will expand on this definition and introduce the different elements that make up a life of Wholebeing.

I introduce this definition of happiness not to challenge, or replace, all other definitions. Instead, the purpose of my definition of happiness as Wholebeing is to operationalize the concept so that it can be used first, to establish a field of happiness studies, and second, to pursue a full and fulfilling life. In other words, the definition is meant to serve as a pragmatic, useful construct, rather than to capture some universal and absolute truth.

*　*　*

The value of focusing on the whole when pursuing the good life is cap-
tured by the ancient Indian fable of *The Blind Men and the Elephant*, a
fable recounted by the nineteenth-century North American poet John
Godfrey Saxe.[7] Six blind men are brought to different parts of an elephant,
and are asked to identify, with their hands, what is in front of them. Each
comes to a radically different verdict: one concludes the elephant must be
a wall; the second that he's touching a spear (really the tusk); while the
others respectively infer that it is a snake, a tree, a fan or a rope. In the final
stanza of the poem, Saxe writes:

> And so these men of Indostan
> Disputed loud and long,
> Each in his own opinion
> Exceeding stiff and strong,
> Though each was partly in the right,
> And all were in the wrong!

The important message in this fable is that understanding only part of
the whole can lead us down the wrong path. Partial truth is no truth. Not
having access to the whole has repercussions beyond epistemology, beyond
the theory of knowledge. For example, if the elephant had been unwell, a
veterinary surgeon would not have been able to help without grasping the
whole. Thinking it were a wall or a rope or any of the other "partial truths"
would be inadequate.

We usually need to know the whole (or as close as we can get) to be
able to bring about health, a notion reflected in some of our languages.
The Latin source of the word *health* is *hal* which means whole. To heal is
to make whole. We find a similarly revealing linguistic connection in
Hebrew, where the word for peace, *shalom* (שלום) comes from the same
root as the word for whole, *shalem* (שלם). In order to bring about peace—
personal inner peace, interpersonal peace, or political peace between
conflicting groups—we need to grasp the whole.

The Xhosa word "Ubuntu" means that each of us is bound up with
everyone else, that we are all part of an interconnected whole. In the
words of Kenyan philosopher and theologian John Mbiti: "I am because
we are; since we are therefore I am."[8] It was the concept of Ubuntu that
provided the architects of post-apartheid South Africa—Nelson Mandela,
Desmond Tutu and others—inspiration and guidance for creating the

rainbow nation, moving from the broken and fragmented past toward a mended and healed future.

Many other cultures around the world and throughout history have valued wholeness as a means of attaining health, peace and other positive outcomes. The ancient Maori legend of New Zealand speaks of the primal parents, Ranginui (the sky father) and Papatūānuku (the earth mother), who remained locked in a passionate embrace that left the world, inhabited by their sons, in perpetual darkness. The strongest of the sons succeeded in prying them apart, and with a vast expanse between them, they grieve for each other, longing to once more unite. Ranginui's tears of sorrow fall toward his beloved in the form of rain. Papatūānuku, in turn, attempts to reach her lover, almost tearing herself apart; and as she sighs, she releases mist toward the sky. It is this perpetual desire to be made whole again that generates humanity's life source.

Thousands of miles from New Zealand, in the Israeli city of Tzfat, the creation myth of Kabbalah was articulated by Rabbi Isaac Luria in the sixteenth century. Kabbalah speaks of the creation of matter from the divine energy of the Almighty. As this energy attempted to fill the vessel of creation with its infinite light, the vessel shattered, sending tiny shards into the world. The shards contain sparks of the original light, and it is humanity's task to gather the shards and release the light within them through good deeds. Once this light is released, the redemption of humankind becomes possible and the divine energy is made whole again.

In the Japanese art of Kintsugi, meaning "golden repair," artisans learn to restore broken pottery with a lacquer mixed with powdered gold—to "heal" it, in a sense, and return it to a state of wholeness. Although the mended object is not a perfect replica of the original, it is still able to serve its purpose because its imperfections were accepted and integrated, not rejected. Kintsugi is a philosophy of life, rather than merely a craft; the process of healing, of being made whole, is encouraged, accentuated and celebrated (see Fig. 2.1).

In our myths, in our art and in our language, we express our longing for wholeness and healing, for ways to mend that which is no longer whole, to reunite the broken aspects of ourselves and the world.

Many people in the modern world recognize this universal yearning. Theologian Thomas Merton reflected in the early twentieth century that, "There is something in the depths of our being that hungers for wholeness."[9] More recently Oprah Winfrey, who has dedicated her life to heal

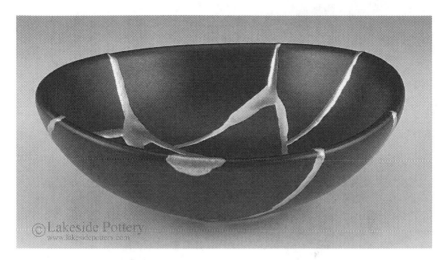

Fig. 2.1 Kintsugi art by Morty Bachar, www.lakesidepottery.com

and to mend, to spread happiness, said that, "The whole point of being alive is to evolve into the complete person you were intended to be."[10]

Peter Senge, senior lecturer at MIT and co-founder of the Society for Organizational Learning, connects the ideas of wholeness and health: "The unhealthiness of our world today is in direct proportion to our inability to see it as a whole."[11] Referring to the story of the blind men and the elephant, Senge notes: "Dividing an elephant in half does not produce two small elephants... Living systems have integrity. Their character depends on the whole. The same is true for organizations; to understand the most challenging managerial issues requires seeing the whole system that generates the issues."[12]

Jack Welch, the legendary CEO of General Electric, has this advice for those who wish to manage: "Face reality as it is, not as it was or as you wish it to be."[13] In order to face reality, you have to understand what reality is; you have to be aware of the full picture. You cannot face the elephant in the room if all you have to go by are unconnected bits and pieces.

Like Welch, psychologist Nathaniel Branden identifies "respect for reality"[14] as a pillar of mental health. Shattering reality without making it whole again shows a blatant disrespect that explains much of the failure of modern psychology. While there has been a great deal of progress in studying mental illness, we nevertheless see a dramatic rise in levels of depression, anxiety and psychological disease. The failure to bring about health and happiness, peace and harmony, is to some extent due to the focus on parts of the human being rather than the whole. A fragmented, dis-integrated reality is an unhealthy reality.

Our academic institutions are not helping mend the situation. In fact, they often contribute to the fragmentation of reality. It is rare to find interdisciplinary and intradisciplinary wholeness in our universities today. The clear and complete division among the disciplines, the meager communication between philosophers and psychologists, artists and scientists, is taking us away from health and peace toward illness and discord. Within disciplines, the situation is no better. The lack of connection among the different psychologies, for example—developmental, cognitive, social and clinical, to mention a few—implies that most psychologists only face part of reality.

As a result of the interdisciplinary and intradisciplinary disconnect, many psychologists fail to adequately comprehend human beings and their needs. By focusing primarily on the brain and ignoring the rest of the body, or by leaving spiritual needs to mystics and intellectual matters to philosophers, psychologists are limited in their ability to treat a human being in the same way blind men may be limited in their ability to treat an elephant. Studying the different parts, and understanding their relationship to the whole, are both necessary to bring about health. Psychology must focus on body just as it does on mind, on spiritual and intellectual wellbeing just as it does on emotional wellbeing.

There is as compelling a need for wholeness in medicine as there is in psychology. While dissecting a particular muscle or cell is necessary and helpful, in research for example, treating an ailment requires an understanding of the whole. As in Kintsugi, we don't stop at the stage when all the pieces are broken; we proceed to gather and mend.

Socrates, considered the father of Western philosophy, pointed out, "The reason why the cure of many diseases is unknown to the physicians of Greece, [is] because they are ignorant of the whole, which ought to be studied also; for the part can never be well unless the whole is well."[15] Knowingly or unknowingly, Socrates was expressing ideas of Eastern philosophers who came before him, like Lao Tzu in China and the Buddha in India. But while Eastern medicine by and large took the idea of wholeness to mind and heart, Western medicine did not. And while Western medicine has certainly advanced remarkably over 2000 years, much more progress is needed—and is within reach. To bring about health, we need to take a "wholistic," interdisciplinary approach, bringing together ancient and modern, cellular and spiritual, mind and body, East and West.

*   *   *

A wholistic approach to happiness implies that we shouldn't merely look at happiness as internally driven. The internal and the external are part of reality, the same whole, and are therefore interconnected: what happens outside impacts, and is in turn impacted by, what happens inside.[16] To understand happiness as Wholebeing, therefore, means that we have to recognize it both as an inside-out phenomenon as well as an outside-in one.

When it comes to inside-out, our personal choices of course play an important role in our happiness. Choosing work or hobbies that are meaningful to us will impact our own happiness, as well as our work and home environments. Choosing to exercise regularly and get sufficient sleep will impact our wellbeing, as well as that of those close to us. And there are many more examples that I address later in the book of how personal choices affect our own as well as others' lives.

At the same time, external circumstances also impact our internal experiences, as demonstrated by the work of political scientist James Fowler and sociologist Nicholas Christakis.[17] Fowler and Christakis discuss the impact of social networks and show that when people socialize together, they influence one another's mental and physical health. Particularly relevant to this discussion is their research on happiness clusters where they illustrate that we're more likely to be happy if we're surrounded by happy friends, and are more likely to be unhappy if those around us are unhappy. Interestingly, happiness is more infectious than unhappiness, so surrounding yourself with happy friends is more important than distancing yourself from unhappy ones.

Other lifestyle choices that directly or indirectly affect our happiness are also impacted by our social environment. It turns out that smoking and obesity are contagious, just as exercising and healthy eating are. It is important to emphasize that social contagion is not deterministic—in other words we're not fated to be obese or unhappy if we are surrounded by obese and unhappy people, just as we're not guaranteed health and happiness if we're in the midst of those who jump for joy.

A wholistic, interconnected reality is one in which an individual is not only impacted by, but also impacts, the collective. A happy person is capable of infecting those around him or her with happiness and even singlehandedly create a happy cluster. A single candle can light up an entire dark room.

Scarcity—the lack, or perceived lack, of a necessary resource— is another aspect of happiness that's both outside-in and inside-out. Research by psychologist Eldar Shafir and economist Sendhil Mullainathan demonstrates how scarcity not only leads to unpleasant feelings, to painful emotions, it also leads to limited and limiting thinking and poor decision making.[18] In other words, scarcity impacts the quality of the choices that people make. Scarcity, therefore, affects happiness levels directly (by causing pain) and indirectly (through poor choices).

Finding ways to reduce scarcity—in the form of poverty and limited access to basic human needs—is of course important to think about, and to do something about, if our concern is a happier world. Those who exit the cycle of poverty will, in all likelihood, become happier; moreover, those who help to alleviate scarcity potentially benefit as well. First, because as scarcity is reduced, there will be more happiness, which is good for all of us given the nature of social contagion. Second, as I will discuss later, giving—being kind and generous—is one of the best ways to increase our own happiness. Alleviating the scarcity of others—helping others—is a significant generator of the ultimate currency, for the person receiving and for the person who gives.

*   *   *

Howard Thurman, the twentieth-century theologian, philosopher and civil-rights activist, was a teacher to millions, including one Martin Luther King. In his book *The Inward Journey*,[19] a collection of meditations addressing the human spirit's deepest needs and hopes, Thurman wrote:

> Thou art made for wholeness,
> Body, mind, spirit: one creative synthesis,
> Moving in perfect harmony within, without,
> With fellow man and nature all around
> To make Heaven where Hell is found.

In these few words, Thurman captures the essence of Wholebeing—the interconnected parts of each of us that make up our whole being, and then our interconnectedness with the outside world as we together make our reality.

To repair ourselves, our organizations and our nations, to advance complex disciplines such as psychology and medicine, we need to shift from the divided to the unified, from the broken to the mended, from the part to the whole. By doing so, we take ourselves and others to a higher, healthier and happier state of being. We heal the world.

NOTES

1. Keller, H. (1957). *The Open Door*. Doubleday.
2. Lyubomirsky, S. (2008). *The How of Happiness: A New Approach to Getting the Life You Want*. Penguin Books.
3. Lakhotia, S. (2012). *Miracles of Health and Happiness*. Diamond Pocket Books.
4. Ibid.
5. Seneca, L. A. (2017). *Morals of a Happy Life, Benefits, Anger and Clemency* (R. L'Estrange, Trans.). Franklin Classics.
6. Ben-Shahar, T. (2007). *Happier: Learn the Secrets to Daily Joy and Lasting Fulfillment*. McGraw-Hill Education.
7. Saxe, J. G. (1872). *The Poems of John Godfrey Saxe*. J. Osgood.
8. Mbiti, J. S. (1969). *African Religions and Philosophy*. Heinemann.
9. Merton, T. (2002). *No Man Is an Island*. Mariner Books.
10. Winfrey, Oprah. What Oprah Knows For Sure About Finding the Courage to Follow Your Dreams. *Oprah.com*. https://www.oprah.com/spirit/what-oprah-knows-for-sure-about-finding-your-dreams (accessed August 15, 2019).
11. Senge, P. M. (2006). *The Fifth Discipline: The Art and Practice of the Learning Organization*. Doubleday.
12. Ibid.
13. Slater, R. (1998). *Jack Welch and the GE Way: Management Insights and Leadership Secrets of the Legendary CEO*. McGraw-Hill.
14. Branden, N. (1995). *The Six Pillars of Self-Esteem: The Definitive Work on Self-Esteem by the Leading Pioneer in the Field*. Bantam.
15. Plato. (2014). *The Dialogues of Plato, Volume 1*. (B. Jowett, Trans.). CreateSpace Independent Publishing.
16. Ross, L. and Nisbett. R. E. (2011). *The Person and the Situation: Perspectives of Social Psychology*. Pinter & Martin.

17. Christakis, N. A. and Fowler, J. H. (2009). *Connected: The Surprising Power of Our Social Networks and How They Shape Our Lives.* Little, Brown and Company.
18. Mullainathan, S. and Shafir, E. (2014). *Scarcity: Why Having Too Little Means So Much.* Picador.
19. Thurman, H. (2007). *The Inward Journey.* Friends United Press. This excerpt is used by permission of Friends United Press. All rights reserved.

CHAPTER 3

The SPIRE of Happiness

To me, the rainbow was a profoundly hopeful symbol, separating the white light of appearances into its multiple spectrum and revealing a hidden dimension. It reminded me of my belief that it was the mission of science to pierce through the layers of everyday reality and penetrate to the truth.
—Candace Pert[1]

To return to The Blind Men and the Elephant fable in the previous chapter: when I recognize that the animal in front of me is an elephant, I've achieved an important first step. But in order to heal it, there is much more I'll need to understand: the nature of its different parts its various systems, organs, tissues, all the way down to the cellular level—and how these parts interact and affect each other. In the same way, defining happiness as the experience of Wholebeing is an important first step that is, in and of itself, not enough. To heal individuals and communities, we need to understand, as much as possible, the parts that make up the whole, and the interrelationships among these parts.

Understanding these complexities is especially important given the paradox inherent in our pursuit of happiness. On the one hand, a great deal of research conducted by psychologists over the past few decades clearly points to the value of cultivating happiness. This value extends beyond the

© The Author(s), under exclusive license to Springer Nature Switzerland AG 2021
T. Ben-Shahar, *Happiness Studies*,
https://doi.org/10.1007/978-3-030-64869-5_3

obvious benefit inherent in the experience of happiness: the fact that it feels good to feel good. Here are just a few examples[2]:

- Increasing happiness improves personal and professional relationships.
- Happiness is associated with a stronger immune system, and happier people live longer.
- Happiness and kindness are intimately linked, in that happiness makes people behave more kindly and generously, and in turn generosity and kindness contribute to happiness.
- In the workplace, a greater sense of wellbeing increases rates of employee retention and engagement, encourages innovation, reduces burnout, and increases both employee productivity and organizational performance.

Given these tangible and measurable benefits of happiness, it would seem natural that we would and should value happiness. On the other hand—and this is where things become complicated and confusing—there is also research suggesting that an overemphasis on happiness could be self-defeating. A study by a University of Denver team in 2011, for example, found that people who place a high value on happiness are more likely to be lonely—a characteristic closely linked to unhappiness or even depression.[3] The study's lead researcher, Iris Mauss, theorized that an intense focus on achieving happiness might lead people to neglect the very parts of their lives—relationships with others or self-care, for example—that could contribute to their happiness.

Is valuing happiness, then, a bad thing? If we don't value it, though, why bother pursuing it? Is self-deception perhaps the way to go? In other words, do we tell ourselves that even though we're dedicating much time to its pursuit, happiness is actually not important to us? We are left with a Shakespearean paradox: To value happiness or not to value happiness, that is the question!

The resolution of the paradox lies in the need to value (and pursue) those elements that *indirectly* lead to happiness. John Stuart Mill, nineteenth-century British philosopher, argued that, "Those only are happy who have their minds fixed on some object other than their own happiness … Aiming thus at something else, they find happiness by the way."[4] What could that "something else" be?

This is where the concept of Wholebeing comes into play, resolving the paradox by shifting our focus from the direct pursuit of happiness to the pursuit of those elements that indirectly lead to happiness. Specifically, each element of Wholebeing—each part that makes up the whole—constitutes an indirect path to the promised land of happiness. What are these elements, these parts, these indirect paths? In keeping with the interdisciplinary nature of happiness studies—bridging East and West, drawing on the works of philosophers, economists, psychologists and biologists—I have come to look at Wholebeing as a multidimensional, multifaceted variable that includes the following parts:

- Spiritual wellbeing
- Physical wellbeing
- Intellectual wellbeing
- Relational wellbeing
- Emotional wellbeing

Together, these five elements form the acronym SPIRE. The various connotations of this word are intimately related to happiness. A spire is "the highest point or summit of something,"[5] just as happiness, being the ultimate currency, is the highest on the hierarchy of goals. A spire also refers to the sprout at the end of a seed when it begins to germinate, leading the rest of the plant upwards through the soil to flourish; likewise, the pursuit of happiness can help us break through boundaries and limitations that hold us back, so that our whole selves can flourish. Finally, the etymological root "spire"—as in *respire* and *inspire*—refers to one's breath or life force; pursuing happiness can inspire us and make us come alive.

* * *

Following is a brief description of each of the SPIRE elements:

- *Spiritual wellbeing.* Most people associate spirituality with religion, specifically with the belief in God. While spirituality can certainly be found in religion, it is possible to travel a spiritual path independent of religion. Spiritual wellbeing refers to the importance of finding a sense of purpose and meaning in life,[6] as well as to elevating ordinary experiences into extraordinary ones through mindful presence.[7]
- *Physical wellbeing.* The understanding that the mind and body are connected—an understanding that challenges a Western approach plagued by dualism—is critical for physical wellbeing. The

psychological and the physical are not two separate and independent entities, but rather connected and interdependent;[8] happiness is not contingent on either the mind or the body, but rather on both.[9] To fulfill our potential for Wholebeing, we need to satisfy our needs for physical exercise, certain nutrients, sleep and touch.[10]

- *Intellectual wellbeing.* While the connection between how intelligent we are and our happiness is ambiguous,[11] there is a strong and definite connection between how we use our intellect and our happiness. Contrary to what legions of well-intentioned educators and parents seem to suggest, a stellar GPA and getting into a top college do not pave the path to happiness. Rather, curiosity and openness,[12] as well as deep engagement in learning,[13] are the building blocks of intellectual wellbeing, and by extension of Wholebeing.
- *Relational wellbeing.* The number one predictor of happiness is not money or prestige, not success or accolades, but the quantity and quality of time we spend with people we care about and who care about us. Healthy relationships constitute the core of a full and fulfilling life.[14] But it's not only our connection to our friends, family or colleagues that matters; cultivating a healthy relationship with our self is essential if we are to enjoy healthy relationships with others.[15]
- *Emotional wellbeing.* Emotions, of course, play an important role in our overall experience of happiness. They inform our thoughts and deeds—and they are the outcomes of our thoughts and deeds. Our emotional wellbeing depends on our ability to both cultivate pleasurable emotions, such as joy and gratitude,[16] as well as deal with painful ones, like envy and sorrow,[17] in a healthy way.

By focusing on the SPIRE elements, each of which indirectly leads to a happier life, we circumvent the trap of the happiness paradox. While highly valuing and directly pursuing happiness can backfire, we can enjoy higher levels of Wholebeing by engaging in work that is personally meaningful (cultivating spiritual wellbeing), exercising regularly and eating healthfully (physical wellbeing), learning continuously (intellectual wellbeing), spending time with a dear friend or family member (relational wellbeing), and writing about our feelings or engaging in fun activities (emotional wellbeing).

*   *   *

The relationship between happiness and the SPIRE elements is analogous to the one between white sunlight and the colors of the rainbow. Happiness is like the bright white light emanating from the sun: pleasant and vital, and yet—as Iris Mauss and her colleagues pointed out—potentially harmful if you focus on it directly.[18] The SPIRE elements are like the colors of the rainbow—beautiful and enticing, and yet not too bright to observe directly. Focusing directly on happiness can be self-defeating, and therefore we apply a prism, employ a lens, that breaks life's ultimate currency into its five SPIRE elements. And it is then that we can, without hurting ourselves, understand, pursue and attain happiness (see Fig. 3.1).

When it comes to the pursuit of happiness, the rainbow is indeed a "profoundly hopeful symbol," as neuroscientist Candace Pert points out. And just as the rainbow reminded Pert of her belief that "it was the mission of science to pierce through the layers of everyday reality and penetrate to the truth," so it can remind us that the mission of happiness studies is to reveal the oft "hidden dimensions" of life's ultimate currency, thus helping us to "penetrate to the truth" of a life well lived.

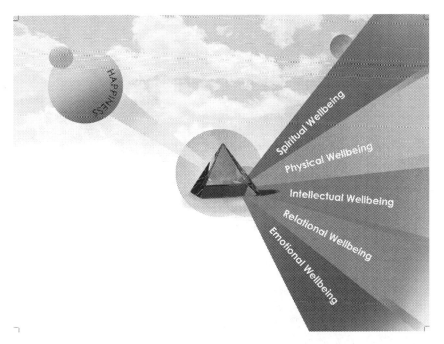

Fig. 3.1   The SPIRE of happiness. (Artwork courtesy of the Happiness Studies Academy)

Just as pure white light is impossible without its spectral components—the colors of the rainbow—each of the five SPIRE elements is essential if we are to adequately define and find happiness. Is happiness about finding a purpose that lends meaning to our life (spiritual wellbeing)? Is it contingent on our experience of health and vitality (physical wellbeing)? Is happiness a function of learning and thinking (intellectual wellbeing)? Does it depend on our interactions with other people (relational wellbeing)? Or is it perhaps about experiencing pleasure (emotional wellbeing)? The answer in each case is "Yes, in part," because all of these are essential elements of Wholebeing. Without meaning and purpose in life, happiness is difficult to sustain.[19] Illness, chronic pain and fatigue often lead to misery.[20] Avoiding thought and contemplation compromises our capacity to lead a full and fulfilling life.[21] Without people we care about and who care about us, we're likely to find ourselves lonely and depressed.[22] A person who experiences little joy, for whom pleasurable emotional experiences are rare, is most certainly unhappy.[23]

Does this mean we should give up on happiness if we don't thrive in all of the SPIRE dimensions? Is it an all-or-nothing proposition, where we either focus on our whole being, or on nothing at all? The answer is no—and this is where the prism analogy reaches its limit. Both sunlight and happiness are made of important, interdependent spectral components—but there's a significant difference. A beam of red or green light is never going to get any whiter without help from the other spectral components; white light requires all of them in combination. Happiness doesn't work that way.

Ideally, we want to cultivate each of the SPIRE elements, but even a single element in any amount can positively impact our overall levels of happiness—our Wholebeing. Introducing physical exercise is an effective way to boost our happiness levels, as is starting to spend more quality time with our nears and dears—and so on for each of the SPIRE elements. We don't need to do it all; small changes can and do make a big difference.

And as we cultivate one, then another, and another of the SPIRE elements, independently or in harmony, we climb higher and higher toward the spire of our being. We lead an inspired life.

*   *   *

As I've presented the SPIRE model to different people—from young students to older parents, from scholars to practitioners—one of the questions that often comes up concerns the role of money in the happiness equation. Why not add financial or material wellbeing to the other SPIRE elements? Why not extend SPIRE to ASPIRE, with Affluential Wellbeing as an integral part of Wholebeing? Money, after all, matters a great deal to our happiness, does it not?

Adding a sixth element to the existing five SPIRE elements is perfectly legitimate, of course, and arguing about what a model of happiness should include and exclude is a good thing rather than a problem. The reason I choose not to include Affluential Wellbeing in my model of happiness is not that I think it's unimportant,[24] but rather because I see it as secondary rather than primary. In other words, spiritual, physical, intellectual, relational and emotional wellbeing are primary human *ends*, and material wellbeing is a secondary *means* toward these ends. Put differently, money plays a supporting role in our pursuit of happiness, potentially contributing to each of the five SPIRE elements.

Here are a few examples, illustrating the role of financial wellbeing in support of the SPIRE elements. Money is necessary to put food on our tables, and supports and contributes to our physical wellbeing.[25] Scarcity, as I pointed out earlier in the book, leads to a great deal of sorrow and anxiety,[26] hence having enough money for our basic needs is important for emotional wellbeing. Fulfillment of our basic material needs is essential if we are to be in the right mindset to learn[27] (intellectual wellbeing) and free to enjoy our family and friends[28] (relational wellbeing). Once basic needs are met, money can still play a role in our happiness levels if we choose to spend it on the right things. For example, when it comes to the ultimate currency, we gain a great deal more if we use money to buy or create meaningful *experiences* (spiritual wellbeing) than if we use it to purchase more *things*.[29]

The distinction between means and ends echoes eighteenth-century German philosopher Immanuel Kant's moral theory.[30] According to Kant, for us to act morally and ascertain right versus wrong, it is important to perceive and consequently treat human beings as ends rather than as means, as valuable in and of themselves, rather than as an instrument for the gratification of our needs: "Act in such a way that you treat humanity, whether in your own person or in the person of another, always at the same time as an end and never simply as a means." Similarly, in the context of a theory of happiness which I'm proposing, the SPIRE elements deserve and receive special status as ends in themselves, and are thereby set apart from other values such as money that, while important, are mere means.

The five SPIRE elements are primary natural needs, essential for fulfilling our potential as human beings. Throughout history, philosophers and psychologists have attempted to define our essential nature, and while individual thinkers and schools of thought do not always agree among themselves, when aggregating their knowledge we come to the SPIRE elements as the essential elements of our nature. Psychologists[31] and philosophers[32] define us as meaning-seeking animals (spiritual); we are, as Aristotle argued,[33] rational animals (intellectual); it is not possible to define us in isolation, as islands[34] (relational); and few would relegate our species to the status of a robot and argue against the notion that feelings and desires define us as human beings[35] (emotional). Finally, the fact that we are defined as this or that kind of animal—spiritual, rational, relational or emotional—implies that our body is too part of our essential nature (physical).

While most people—including the great philosophers and psychologists—would agree that money plays an important role in our overall wellbeing, few, even among the economists, would argue that we are financial animals. And if you are among those who beg to differ and believe that including money as a primary end in a theory of happiness can help you better understand, pursue and attain Wholebeing, then by all means, ASPIRE or FSPIRE is the model for you.

*   *   *

I would like to bring the idea of Wholebeing to life through a personal example. Friday-night meals at my parents' house with my extended family are, for me, a great source of the five SPIRE elements.

Most weeks, my parents, my wife and children, my siblings and their families are all there, and I experience a deep sense of meaning spending time with the most beloved people in my life. Moreover, the parts of the ceremony—including blessing over the wine and the bread, singing songs to welcome the Sabbath, and participating in other rituals that have been passed down from generation to generation—together constitute a *spiritual* experience.

The experience of the Friday-night meal is also a *physical* one. My mom's food is spectacular, both delicious and healthy, and my brother usually makes us laugh so hard that it feels like an ab workout. The abundance of hugs and kisses contribute to the experience of physical wellbeing.

Beyond the tasty food, there is also plenty of food for thought, making our experience an *intellectual* feast as well. Though we often speak during the week about everyday matters, on Friday night we share deeper ideas and thoughts relating to philosophy, politics, education and more. Usually my mom or my brother prepares a short, thought-provoking sermon relating a topic from the Bible to our lives, connecting ancient wisdom to modern living. My dad, who is a fountain of knowledge, can always be relied upon for fascinating discussions and enlightening stories. I almost always leave the meal feeling intellectually nourished, having learned something new or been provoked to further explore an idea we discussed.

Not surprisingly, the *relational* experience stands out on Friday nights. The way I feel after spending hours with the people I care about most in the world is, for me, living proof that the number one predictor of happiness is time we spend with people we care about and who care about us. Essentially, whenever I spend uninterrupted time with my family or my friends, my Wholebeing quotient goes up significantly.

At these Friday meals, the spiritual, physical, intellectual and relational elements combine to ensure the experience is a deeply *emotional* one. Our time together is filled with joy and fun and love. At the same time, it's a safe space for all of us to share difficulties, to give voice to our sorrow or pain or sadness.

Is every Friday night a peak experience for me? No. There are times when I'm very tired, or something is weighing on me, and I'm unable to be fully present. Sometimes another family member is going through a hardship, and that naturally affects us all. However, time and again, these regular get-togethers provide my family and me with a profound experience of Wholebeing.

I use these family meals as an example because of their extraordinariness: It's possible to experience Wholebeing—enjoying spiritual, physical, intellectual, relational and emotional wellbeing—all in a single evening. But it doesn't happen every Friday for my family, and there is no need to despair if most or all of our experiences fall short of delivering the full SPIRE spectrum. It is perfectly fine, and wonderful, to go through an entire day and experience some, not all, of the elements of Wholebeing. We can enjoy an abundance of happiness in smaller doses over a longer period, from a month to a lifetime, knowing that each time we cultivate one of the SPIRE elements, we brighten up our life, and spread light.

NOTES

1. Pert, C. B. (1999). *Molecules of Emotion: The Science Behind Mind-Body Medicine.* Simon & Schuster.
2. Lyubomirsky, S., King, L. and Diener, E. (2005). The Benefits of Frequent Positive Affect: Does Happiness Lead to Success? *Psychological Bulletin, 131*, 803–855.

Diener, E. and Tay, L. (2017). A Scientific Review of the Remarkable Benefits of Happiness for Successful and Healthy Living. In *Happiness: Transforming the Development Landscape*. Centre for Bhutan Studies and GNH.

3. Mauss, I. B., Tamir, M., Anderson, C. L. and Savino, N. S. (2011). Can seeking happiness make people unhappy? Paradoxical effects of valuing happiness. *Emotion, 11*, 807–815.

4. Mill, J. S. (2018). *Autobiography*. Loki's Publishing.

5. Spire. (2019). In *Dictionary.com*. https://www.dictionary.com/browse/spire?s=t (accessed August 15, 2019).

6. Frankl, V. (2006). *Man's Search for Meaning*. Beacon Press.

7. Hanh, T. N. (1999). *The Miracle of Mindfulness: An Introduction to the Practice of Meditation* (M. Ho, Trans.). Beacon Press.

8. Damasio, A. (2006). *Descartes' Error: Emotion, Reason, and the Human Brain*. Vintage Books.

9. Kabat-Zinn, J. (2013). *Full Catastrophe Living: Using the Wisdom of Your Body and Mind to Face Stress, Pain, and Illness*. Bantam.

10. Ratey, J. J. (2015). *Go Wild: Eat Fat, Run Free, Be Social and Follow Evolution's Other Rules for Total Health and Wellbeing*. Little, Brown and Company.

11. Raghunathan, R. (2016). *If You're So Smart Why Aren't You Happy?* Portfolio.

Dimitrijevic, A. A., Marjanovic, Z. J. and Dimitrijevic, A. (2018). Whichever Intelligence Makes You Happy: The Role of Academic, Emotional, and Practical Abilities in Predicting Psychological Well-Being. *Personality and Individual Differences, 132*, 6–13.

12. Kashdan, T. B. (2010). *Curiosity: The Missing Ingredient to a Fulfilling Life*. Harper Perennial.

13. Csikszentmihalyi, M. (2014). *Applications of Flow in Human Development and Education: The Collected Works of Mihaly Csikszentmihalyi*. Springer.

14. Waldinger, R. (2015). What Makes a Good Life? Lessons From the Longest Study on Happiness. *Ted.com*. https://www.ted.com/talks/robert_waldinger_what_makes_a_good_life_lessons_from_the_longest_study_on_happiness (accessed August 20, 2019).

15. Harris, M. A. and Orth, U. (2019). The Link Between Self-Esteem and Social Relationships: A Meta-Analysis of Longitudinal Studies. *Journal of Personality and Social Psychology*.

16. Emmons, R. (2008). *Thanks: How Practicing Gratitude Can Make You Happier*. Mariner Books.

17. Biswas-Diener, R. and Kashdan, T. B. (2014). *The Upside of Your Dark Side: Why Being Your Whole Self—Not Just Your "Good" Self—Drives Success and Fulfillment*. Plume.

18. Mauss, I. B., Tamir, M., Anderson, C. L. and Savino, N. S. (2011). Can seeking happiness make people unhappy? Paradoxical effects of valuing happiness. *Emotion, 11,* 807–815.
19. McKnight, P. E. and Kashdan, T. B. (2009). Purpose in Life as a System that Creates and Sustains Health and Well-Being: An Integrative, Testable Theory. *Review of General Psychology, 13,* 242–251.
20. Simons, L., Elman, I. and Borsook, D. (2014). Psychological Processing in Chronic Pain: A Neural Systems Approach. *Journal of Neuroscience & Biobehavioral Reviews, 39,* 61–78.
    Walker, M. (2018). *Why We Sleep: Unlocking the Power of Sleep and Dreams.* Scribner.
21. Aristotle. (1954). *The Nicomachean Ethics* (D. Ross, Trans.). Oxford University Press.
22. Cacioppo, S., Capitanio, J. P. and Cacioppo, J. T. (2014). Toward a Neurology of Loneliness. *Psychological Bulletin, 140,* 1464–1504.
23. Ben-Shahar, T. (2007). *Happier: Learn the Secrets to Daily Joy and Lasting Fulfillment.* McGraw-Hill Education.
24. Dunn, E. and Norton, M. (2013). *Happy Money: The Science of Happier Spending.* Simon & Schuster.
25. Verfaillie, N. (2013). 10 Facts About Poverty and Malnutrition. *The Borgen Project.* https://borgenproject.org/10-facts poverty-malnutrition/ (accessed August 17, 2019).
26. Mullainathan, S. and Shafir, E. (2014). *Scarcity: Why Having Too Little Means So Much.* Picador.
27. Jensen, E. (2009). *Teaching With Poverty in Mind: What Being Poor Does to Kids' Brains and What Schools Can Do About It.* ASCD.
28. Gibb, J., Rix, K., Wallace, E., Fitzsimons, E. and Mostafa, T. (2016). *Poverty and Children's Personal and Social Relationships.* National Children's Bureau and Centre for Longitudinal Studies.
29. Dunn, E. and Norton, M. (2013). *Happy Money: The Science of Happier Spending.* Simon & Schuster.
30. Kant, I. (1989). *Foundations of the Metaphysics of Morals.* Pearson.
31. Frankl, V. (2006). *Man's Search for Meaning.* Beacon Press.
    Yalom, I. (1980). *Existential Psychotherapy.* Basic Books.
32. Nozick, R. (1990). *The Examined Life: Philosophical Meditations.* Simon & Schuster.
    McPherson, D. (Ed.). (2017). *Spirituality and the Good Life: Philosophical Approaches.* Cambridge University Press.
33. Aristotle. (1954). *The Nicomachean Ethics* (D. Ross, Trans.). Oxford University Press.
34. Merton, T. (2002). *No Man Is an Island.* Mariner Books.
35. Damasio, A. (2006). *Descartes' Error: Emotion, Reason, and the Human Brain.* Vintage Books.

CHAPTER 4

The Twelve Principles of Happiness

A principle is an abstraction which subsumes a great number of concretes. It is only by means of principles that one can set one's long-range goals and evaluate the concrete alternatives of any given moment.
—Ayn Rand[1]

At the core of the interdisciplinary field of happiness studies are twelve principles that provide a deeper understanding of the Wholebeing approach and the five SPIRE elements. In this chapter I explain why it is important to have principles—be it for creating an academic program or for experiencing and fostering Wholebeing—and then briefly introduce each of them.

Principles are the underlying ideas, the fundamental tenets of a system of thought or belief, and so provide the basis for its design and structure. Principles define a system, and by doing so become gatekeepers, deciding what is and is not included within the system. To use a concrete metaphor of a building, principles provide the design for the building and set the boundaries of its structure. By doing so, principles designate what is inside the structure, and what remains outside.

Why, though, do we need gatekeepers to happiness? If we accept that there are many roads to happiness, why impose structural boundaries for inclusion and exclusion? Because without principles, a system becomes diluted and meaningless. If there are no discriminating principles, then

T. Ben-Shahar, *Happiness Studies*,
https://doi.org/10.1007/978-3-030-64869-5_4

anything goes; everything is as important as everything else—which implies that nothing is important.

Think about it: In a world where everything is blue, there is no blue; we need to distinguish blue from other colors to understand what blue is. Similarly, in a world where every idea and practice is Wholebeing, there is no Wholebeing. Explicit principles furnish us with the ability to distinguish the ideas and practices that lead to Wholebeing from those that do not; they help us to discriminate between the relevant and the irrelevant, for the purpose of understanding, pursuing and attaining happiness.

Here's an analogy from the field of mathematics, which is governed by principles in the forms of axioms, theorems and laws. One of the simplest is the Commutative Law of Addition, which tells us that $A + B = B + A$. Replacing the Commutative Law of Addition with an alternative law such as $A + B = A - B$ would define a new system or field of study. Whatever $A + B = A - B$ represents, it's not math as we know it and study it. Mathematics remains coherent and useful precisely by excluding $A + B = A - B$ from entering the gated structure of the field.

Another analogy is a national constitution, which provides guidelines for the construction of a country's governance: what is allowed and what isn't. A constitution expresses the fundamental laws from which other laws are derived, and provides the standard by which human activities are either accepted as lawful or rejected as unlawful. That is to say, it establishes the principles of the society. While interpretations of a part of the constitution can vary, the constitution is still the basis of the disagreement, and it is not taken lightly. The government and the courts are dedicated to upholding it.

The twelve principles are to happiness studies what axioms, theorems and laws are to math, and what a constitution is to a nation. Made explicit, the happiness studies principles become a guide for further research and study. No less important, these principles allow us, in the words of philosopher Ayn Rand, to "evaluate the concrete alternatives of any given moment"[2] and chart our path toward a more wholesome, happier life.

* * *

Following are the twelve principles. The first two, Wholebeing Principles 1 and 2, are overarching principles that establish the foundation of the field of happiness studies. The remaining ten principles follow from these two fundamental premises, laying out a more detailed guide for understanding and pursuing happiness. The ten divide equally among the five SPIRE elements—two for each element—and elaborate on the brief descriptions I've offered in the previous chapter.

The Twelve Principles of the Wholebeing Approach

- Wholebeing 1 (W1)
  The aim of life is and ought to be wholeperson wellbeing

- Wholebeing 2 (W2)
  Everything is interconnected

- Spiritual 1 (S1)
  A purposeful life is a spiritual life

- Spiritual 2 (S2):
  The ordinary is elevated to the extraordinary through mindful presence

- Physical 1 (P1)
  Mind and body are connected

- Physical 2 (P2)
  A healthy life requires adherence to our given nature

- Intellectual 1 (I1)
  Curiosity and openness help us make the most of what life has
  to offer

- Intellectual 2 (I2)
  Engaging in deep learning fulfills our potential as rational animals

- Relational 1 (R1)
  Relationships are crucial for a full and fulfilling life

- Relational 2 (R2):
  The foundation of healthy relationships with others is a healthy
  relationship with oneself

- Emotional 1 (E1)
  All emotions are legitimate, acceptable, part of being human

- Emotional 2 (E2):
  Emotions are the outcome of our thoughts and deeds and inform
  our thoughts and deeds

- Wholebeing 1 (W1)
The aim of life is and ought to be wholeperson wellbeing

Whether consciously or subconsciously, explicitly or implicitly, by our very nature we pursue happiness—not just happiness as pleasure or satisfaction, but happiness in the sense of Wholebeing, where we look for a spiritually meaningful, physically healthy, intellectually stimulating, interpersonally connected, as well as emotionally pleasurable existence.

The first Wholebeing principle, or some variation of it, has been articulated by philosophers and theologians, far and wide—from Aristotle to Helen Keller, from Lao Tzu to the Dalai Lama. In his landmark book *The Varieties of Religious Experience,* North American philosopher and psychologist William James wrote: "If we were to ask the question: 'What is human life's chief concern?' one of the answers we should receive would be: 'It is happiness.' How to gain, how to keep, how to recover happiness, is in fact for most men at all times the secret motive of all they do, and of all they are willing to endure."[3]

But the fact that happiness *is* our aim, does not automatically imply that it *ought* to be so.[4] In other words, just because most of us situate happiness as the highest on the hierarchy of goals, doesn't necessarily mean that it is a good thing that we do. The first principle stipulates that we ought to pursue Wholebeing, because of the clear evidence that doing so is good for the individual and society.

In a review of the research on wellbeing, psychologists Sonja Lyubomirsky, Laura King, and Ed Diener note that "Numerous studies show that happy individuals are successful across multiple life domains, including marriage, friendship, income, work performance, and health."[5] Given all these benefits, the real question is why ought we not pursue happiness? The primary opposition to the value of pursuing happiness stems from the belief that benefit to self and benefit to others are in conflict. According to this reasoning, the pursuit of personal happiness is pitted against others' happiness—so if I pursue and attain more happiness for myself, the argument goes, I'm necessarily depriving others of the same currency. An increasing amount of research, however, points to the fact that pursuing happiness, defined as Wholebeing, sets up a win-win situation, a positive rather than a negative sum game.

There is a positive upward spiral between happiness and goodness.[6] For example, when we are generous toward others we feel better,[7] and when we feel better we are more likely to be generous;[8] similarly, giving to others is a powerful generator of health[9] (physical wellbeing) as well as meaning in life[10] (spiritual wellbeing), and we are much more likely to give to others when we are in good health and leading a meaningful life.[11]

Happiness is a worthy aim to pursue, first because we benefit from it personally, and second because by doing so we are more likely to contribute to a happier, healthier and better world.

*   *   *

- Wholebeing 2 (W2)
  Everything is interconnected

This principle summons us to take a systemic rather than a symptomatic view of the world, and of our lives in it. Each of us is a whole being, composed of interconnected parts, that is in turn part of a larger whole. This echoes our discussion about the importance of wholeness: Learning to see ourselves and the world as an interconnected whole is critical for physical and psychological health, for peace as an individual and as a collective. In an essay titled "It's An Interconnected World," organizational behaviorist Margaret Wheatley writes: "I believe that our very survival depends upon us becoming better systems thinkers."[12]

On the individual level, understanding the interconnectedness of the SPIRE elements and their collective impact on our Wholebeing is important if we are to lead a full and fulfilling life. Take, for example, a person who decides to live a life of a hedonist, focusing on whatever provides her with pleasure (emotional wellbeing) while forgoing a sense of purpose (spiritual wellbeing). This person is unlikely to enjoy a deep sense of happiness, nor be able to sustain long-term happiness.[13] Similarly, a person who constantly exercises his mind (intellectual wellbeing) but neglects his body (physical wellbeing) significantly compromises his potential not only for physical health but also for mental health.[14] The same applies to all five SPIRE elements—compromising one is compromising the whole.

On the societal level, understanding our interconnectedness with other people and our environment is critical—for the world and for us as individuals. The poet T. S. Eliot claimed that "Hell is the place where nothing connects."[15] Could it be, then, that heaven is a place where everything connects?

There is a popular parable common to several faith traditions that describes hell as a place where people are sitting around a large table with delicious food and sumptuous options. And yet, the inhabitants are famished, suffering from hunger, because the spoons they were given are longer than their arms and they're unable to enjoy any of the food in front of them. Heaven could be the same place—with the same food and the same spoons—but where the inhabitants feed each other. They celebrate, rather than ignore, their interdependence.

*   *   *

- Spiritual 1 (S1)
A purposeful life is a spiritual life

This principle challenges the monopoly of religion on spirituality, and while it acknowledges that religion can and often does provide us with spiritual wellbeing, it also points out ways through which we can find spirituality elsewhere in our life. The *Oxford English Dictionary* defines spirituality as "the real sense of significance of something."[16] We can infuse meaning and significance—a sense of purpose—into almost everything we do, and by doing so turn everyday activities into spiritual experiences. An investment banker who finds a sense of purpose in her work, who sees her work as significant, leads a more spiritual and fulfilling life than a monk who is unable to connect to the real significance of his daily rituals.

Following the Second World War, father of Logotherapy Viktor Frankl wrote about an *existential vacuum* that he perceived among his students, something that he had never seen to that extent.[17] Today, the situation is even worse, especially for the young members of our society. In his book, *Path to Purpose*, Stanford Professor William Damon points out, "The most pervasive problem of the day is a sense of emptiness that has ensnared many young people … apathy and anxiety have become the dominant moods, and disengagement or even cynicism has replaced the natural hopefulness of youth."[18] Without a sense of purpose, young people are unlikely to experience happiness; tragically, without a sense of purpose, older people are more likely to die. As Damon concludes: "Study after study has found a person's sense of life purpose to be closely connected to virtually all dimensions of wellbeing."

A purpose doesn't have to be earth shattering or grandiose. One person may find deciphering ancient texts from a lost civilization to be meaningful, while another may find significance in raising a family; a person may find purpose in teaching a small class in a small town, and someone else may find serving food in a soup kitchen personally fulfilling; and there are those for whom trading stocks or writing political editorials is meaningful. Many people, of course, find a sense of purpose in their lives—and hence spirituality—through religion and the belief in God. A goal or an activity becomes purposeful—a spiritual experience—when it is significant and meaningful.

*   *   *

- Spiritual 2 (S2):
  The ordinary is elevated to the extraordinary through mindful presence

While stipulating the need for purpose and significance, the first spiritual principle still implicitly limits what we ought to describe as "spiritual"; it's a word reserved for activities pregnant with meaning. The second principle does away with any barriers to entry, claiming that we can experience anything we do as spiritual. To be experienced as spiritual, an activity does not need to be rendered meaningful and significant from the outside in; virtually any experience already possesses an inherent value and thus can be made extraordinary from the inside out. As author Henry Miller writes, "The moment one gives close attention to any thing, even a blade of grass, it becomes a mysterious, awesome, indescribably magnificent world in itself."[19]

In 1999, a leading scholar in the field of positive psychology, Mihaly Csikszentmihalyi, asked a simple question: "If we are so rich, why aren't we happy?"[20] Csikszentmihalyi was alluding to the research demonstrating that even though our generation is wealthier than previous ones, we are not happier for it. In fact, while levels of material prosperity are on the rise, so are levels of depression and anxiety. Tara Bennet-Goleman, a psychotherapist who has done much to bring together Eastern and Western psychologies, provides an eloquent answer to Csikszentmihalyi's question, explaining why our growing wealth is not translated into an increase in happiness—and what we can do to change that:

The richest banquet, the most exotic travel, the most interesting, attractive lover, the finest home—all of these experiences can seem somehow unrewarding and empty if we don't really attend to them fully—if our minds are elsewhere, preoccupied with disturbing thoughts. By the same token, the simplest of life's pleasures—eating a piece of fresh-baked bread, seeing a work of art, spending moments with a loved one—can be amply rich if we bring a full attention to them. The remedy to dissatisfaction is inside us, in our minds, not in groping for new and different outer sources of satisfaction.[21]

By being mindful and present regularly and consistently—whether through formal or informal meditation—we increase our spiritual wellbeing and overall happiness. When we move through the world aware of what is here and now, the ordinary becomes extraordinary, the mundane sacred. Paying attention to our breath, observing a flame, savoring the taste of a fresh strawberry, feeling our body as we walk—these experiences are the very ingredients of a spiritually rich life. In the words of Buddhist monk Thich Nhat Hanh: "At any moment, you have a choice, that either leads you closer to your spirit or further away from it."[22]

*   *   *

- Physical 1 (P1)
Mind and body are connected

When the seventeenth-century French philosopher René Descartes famously wrote "*Cogito, ergo sum*" ("I think, therefore I am"),[23] he was beginning to develop his theory of *dualism*, the idea that mind and body are two distinct and irreconcilable entities. Despite the fact that Descartes never came up with a good explanation for *why* or *how* the mind caused the body to do things, or for *why* or *how* our physical state affected our mental state, his theory nevertheless had a deep impact on Western philosophy and medicine. The first physical principle challenges the dualistic mindset, the belief that mind and body can be pulled apart.

The physical and psychological price of dualism is high. The attempt to heal the body independent of the mind is unlikely to lead to optimal health; and trying to heal the mind without paying attention to the body compromises on our happiness. There is ample research demonstrating how the mind affects the body. Take the placebo effect, for example.[24] A fake drug can alleviate our headache and a mock procedure can heal our sore knee—because we believe that they will. Other research shows that cognitive behavioral therapy or a mindfulness intervention can alleviate back pain, no less so than physical therapy.[25]

The impact of body over mind is also as clear as night follows day. The psychological benefits of physical exercise[26] or healthy eating[27] or touch[28] clearly demonstrate the inseparable link between the two entities Descartes perceived as distinct. As the Latin route of the word "health" suggests, we need Wholistic Medicine and we need Wholistic Psychology if we are to fulfill our potential for health.

Jon Kabat-Zinn, creator of the Mindfulness-Based Stress Reduction (MBSR) program, writes: "Perhaps the most fundamental development in behavioral medicine is the recognition that we can no longer think about health as being solely a characteristic of the body or the mind because body and mind are interconnected."[29] The wholistic mindset that integrates mind and body is the path to fulfilling our potential for both health and happiness.

*   *   *

- Physical 2 (P2)
A healthy life requires adherence to our given nature

The philosophical root of the second physical premise can be traced to British philosopher Francis Bacon, a contemporary of René Descartes. Bacon argued that to bring about progress and channel nature's potential for our own purposes, we must first accept reality. It is only when we accept nature's laws and processes—when we come to terms with their existence rather than perceive them as alterable—that we can make productive use of them. With his claim that "nature to be commanded must be obeyed,"[30] Bacon laid the philosophical foundation for modern science.

The birth of the scientific revolution, which in turn gave rise to the industrial revolution and to unprecedented material affluence, came about when people followed Bacon's advice and obeyed the laws of nature. Implicit in Bacon's call for obeying nature's laws are two separate steps: first, understanding nature, and second, adhering to it. For example, it was only after first understanding and then, second, adhering to the law of gravity and the laws of thermodynamics, that people were able to construct flying machines and attain other engineering feats. An engineer who either does not understand the natural laws or understands them and chooses to turn to wishful or magical thinking is unlikely to succeed in unearthing the potential inherent in reality.

Similarly, in order to fulfill the potential inherent in our bodies—to experience physical wellbeing—we first have to understand, and second to adhere to, our natural physical needs. Modern science and medicine are revealing to us more ways to care for our bodies and satisfy our natural needs, bringing us closer to optimal functioning.[31]

Regular physical exercise, for instance, has the same effect on our psychological wellbeing as our most powerful psychiatric medication. Conforming to nature's call for regular rest and recovery—in the form of sufficient sleep, as an example—is critical for mental health (being a powerful antidote for depression and anxiety) and physical health (at times making the difference between life and death). And when it comes to nutrition, the closer we are to nature in our preferences—choosing natural food over processed food—the longer and better we will live. By adhering to nature's command, you can, in the words of *National Geographic* researcher Dan Buettner, "add years to your life and life to your years."[32]

*   *   *

- Intellectual 1 (I1)
  Curiosity and openness help us make the most of what life has to offer

Curiosity (the desire to learn) and openness to experience (the desire to do) are essential if we are to fulfill our Wholebeing potential.[33] We are born curious and open, with a deep-seated desire to learn about the world. This love of learning rarely dies, but it sometimes lies dormant, awaiting awakening. To resurrect it, we need to ask more and explore more, try out and reach out, even after we strike out.

One of the barriers standing in the way of rekindling the love of learning is the false belief that some people are simply not curious or open—that, for one reason or another, they have permanently lost their desire to learn and grow. But to categorically state "I don't like learning" is analogous to declaring "I don't like eating." We might not like sardines or cucumbers, but we are so constituted that we derive pleasure from eating, at least some things. Similarly, we might not like studying calculus or ancient languages, but our nature dictates that we are capable of deriving pleasure from learning some things. And just as food is necessary for survival, and hence our constitution is such that we desire it, so is learning and growing necessary for survival and hence we naturally crave it. Actively indulging our curiosity and opening ourselves up to different experiences feed our inquisitive nature just as food and water feed our physical nature.

Author and civil rights activist Lillian Smith wrote: "When you stop learning, stop listening, stop looking and asking questions, always new questions, then it is time to die."[34] In fact, learning new things not only contributes to psychological health and happiness, but also to physical health and longevity. Psychologist Laura Carstensen, director of the Stanford Center on Longevity, has said, "I think most social scientists would put their money on education as the most important factor in ensuring longer lives."[35]

*   *   *

- Intellectual 2 (I2)
Engaging in deep learning fulfills our potential as rational animals

There is a common misconception that an ideal life could be the life of a grazing cow—limited in scope and focus, unburdened and simple. But because of our unique nature we need more than a full stomach to experience fulfillment. Aristotle defines a human being as a *rational animal*,[36] suggesting that the faculty that thinks, contemplates and reflects distinguishes us from other species. While we certainly pay a price for this faculty—life would have been simpler had Adam and Eve not tasted from the tree of knowledge—there is no turning back. Our nature is such that to fulfill our potential we need to exercise our intellect, and doing so requires conscious and concerted effort. As Abigail Adams noted, "Learning is not to be attained by chance, it must be sought with ardor and attended to with diligence."[37]

Exercising our intellectual capacities is not about achieving great heights or becoming all that we can become. The second intellectual principle refers to a process rather than outcome, to applying our capacities rather than achieving measurable results. Even if we have the potential to become a world-renowned scholar or the president of our country, we could still be happy reading and re-reading poetry or frequenting a local art museum. Becoming a famous scholar or a president are *external* manifestations of potential, whereas Wholebeing is a function of *internal* application of potential—and there is no connection between external measures of success and deep, lasting happiness.[38] An essential element of Wholebeing is experiencing the satisfaction that comes from using our intellectual capacities fully and well.

One of the most harmful afflictions of the modern world is the widespread practice of surfing and skimming, and the near-universal neglect of the deep dive. Closely studying a text or nature, delving into the depths of a math problem or closely listening to a piano concerto, trying to better understand the complexities of a social situation or learning a dance choreography—these are all ways of cultivating intellectual wellbeing.[39] Twentieth-century British philosopher Bertrand Russell wrote that "the happiness that is genuinely satisfying is accompanied by the fullest exercise of our faculties and the fullest realization of the world in which we live."[40]

* * *

- Relational 1 (R1)
Relationships are crucial for a full and fulfilling life

Investing in relationships, spending time with people we care about and who care about us, yields the highest return in the ultimate currency. The happiest (and healthiest) individuals in the world are ones who spend time with people they care about and who care about them.[41] The happiest nations in the world are not the wealthiest nations, but rather ones where there is an emphasis on social relations.[42] As Francis Bacon pointed out in the early seventeenth century, "Friendship redoubleth joys and cutteth griefs in half."[43]

The two criteria for fulfilling the latent potential within our connection to other people are making relationships a *priority* and making them *real*. For more and more people, career and money have become the primary criteria for success, and they are replacing relationships as the top priority. People whose number one goal is to make money are on average less happy than others—this finding holds true for the general population as well as for business school students.[44] There is of course nothing wrong with striving for material success and financial security, but we pay a psychological price when it comes at the expense of the most significant generator of happiness. In the words of Eric Klinenberg,[45] a sociology professor at New York University: "Social relationships are a powerful predictor of happiness—much more so than money. Happy people have extensive social networks and good relationships with the people in those networks."

The second criterion for deriving the potential from relationships is that they are real. Virtual social networks today often take the place of actual social gatherings, and while there are numerous benefits to these networks, they are not enough. One thousand virtual friends are no substitute for that one intimate friend; social media is no substitute for face-to-face interactions. The increase in the amount of time we spend interacting with others through screens also explains the increase in loneliness levels—which is, among other things, associated with depression and heart disease. Klinenberg notes that "The greater the proportion of online interaction [versus face-to-face interaction] the lonelier you are."[46] As appealing as online interactions are, we sometimes need to disconnect in order to connect.

*   *   *

- Relational 2 (R2):
The foundation of healthy relationships with others is a healthy relationship with oneself

When the Dalai Lama and some of his followers began to work with European and American scientists, they were surprised to hear from them that self-hate was a common phenomenon in the West.[47] The absence of self-love—the pervasiveness of low levels of self-esteem—is at least in part a result of the split between self-love and love for others. After all, if love for self (selfish or egoistic love) comes at the expense of love for others (selfless or altruistic love), then a conscientious person is likely to choose to forgo self-love, or at the very least be plagued by guilt.

The discrepancy that is so ingrained in the West, simply does not exist in Tibetan thought. The word *tsewa* is Tibetan for compassion and caring, and it refers equally to self and others. In the words of the Dalai Lama, "Compassion, or *tsewa*, as it is understood in the Tibetan tradition, is a state of mind or way of being where you extend how you relate to yourself toward others as well."[48] Not only does the Tibetan understanding of compassion not negate self-love; it elevates it as the primary form of love, a precondition for the love of others: "Yourself first, and then in a more advanced way the aspiration will embrace others. In a way, high levels of compassion are nothing but an advanced state of that self-interest. That's why it is hard for people who have a strong sense of self-hatred to have genuine compassion toward others. There is no anchor, no basis to start from."[49] The Dalai Lama is essentially describing how starting with self-love does not only lead to happier individuals, it leads to happier relationships—and by extension, a happier society.

On the physical level it's easier to see the link between taking care of oneself and taking care of others. A mother needs to nourish herself if she is to nourish her baby. Each time we get on a plane we're reminded that in case of emergency we must first put the oxygen mask on ourselves, before putting one on others—because if we fail to take care of ourselves, we'll not only hurt ourselves but also fail to take care of others. The exact same principle applies to the realm of relationships: self-love is a prerequisite for loving others. As Eleanor Roosevelt pointed out: "Friendship with one's self is all important, because without it, one cannot be friends with anyone else in the world."[50]

Whenever we nurture ourselves, our capacity for giving and receiving grows, and hence our relationships are bound to grow. While numerous Western thinkers throughout the ages have pitted selfishness and egoism against selflessness and altruism, the Wholebeing approach recognizes our interdependence and thus calls for a reintegration of self and others.

*   *   *

- Emotional 1 (E1)
  All emotions are legitimate, acceptable, part of being human

It seems obvious to most people that emotions play a significant role in our happiness, since we so often evaluate how happy or unhappy we are based on our emotional state. And while the Wholebeing approach argues for a deeper and broader view of happiness than the one that equates happiness with pleasurable emotions, there is no questioning the fact that emotions do indeed constitute a central pillar of Wholebeing.

Focusing on the cultivation of pleasurable emotions like joy, love, amusement, inspiration, serenity and gratitude is of course vital for happiness.[51] At the same time, appreciating and embracing painful emotions like anger, sadness, anxiety and envy is no less important.[52] And yet, not all emotions are treated equally; emotions on the painful side of the spectrum are frequently discriminated against. The fact that so many people refer to painful emotions as *negative* emotions points to the pervasive and harmful attitude toward them.

One of the major obstacles to becoming happier is the belief that life can and ought to be free of painful emotions. When we dismiss painful emotions as negative, when we do what we can to avoid them and reject them, we pay a high price. First, when we avoid or run away from emotionally challenging experiences, we compromise on our potential for learning and growing, as well as for success. While painful emotions are, by definition, unpleasant, most of us looking back on our lives would admit that at least some of the hardship we experienced along the way was a blessing.

Second, by rejecting painful emotions we actually end up experiencing more pain than is necessary or warranted by the situation. This paradox— that the rejection of painful emotions leads to their escalation—occurs because emotions need an outlet, to be expressed somehow, and cannot be kept under arrest, suppressed, for long. When we reject painful emotions, they overstay their welcome.[53] In contrast, when we release and experience them—by talking or writing about them,[54] by crying or mindfully observing them[55]—they stay for as short as possible and as long as necessary.

The third outcome of rejecting painful emotions is that we forgo our potential to experience pleasurable emotions. All of our feelings flow along the same emotional pipeline, so when we block painful emotions, we are also indirectly blocking pleasurable ones. In the words of Golda Meir, "Those who don't know how to weep with their whole heart don't know how to laugh either."[56] More generally, it is when we open ourselves up to unhappiness that we usher in happiness.

Painful emotions, like pleasurable ones, are an inevitable part of the experience of being human, and therefore rejecting them is ultimately rejecting part of our humanity. To lead a full and fulfilling life—to realize our potential for Wholebeing—we need to give ourselves the permission to be human.[57]

* * *

- Emotional 2 (E2)

Emotions are the outcome of our thoughts and deeds, and inform our thoughts and deeds

The second emotional principle is a manifestation of the second Wholebeing principle (W2) regarding the interconnectedness of all things. Our emotions, thoughts and deeds are part of one system, as they affect and are affected by one another. A key insight from systems thinking is that once we understand the interconnectedness among the different elements of a system, we can identify the levers for change. Peter Senge writes that "The bottom line of systems thinking is leverage—seeing where actions and changes in structures can lead to significant, enduring improvements."[58] In the context of the second emotional principle, our thoughts and our deeds, what we think and what we do, are important leverage points for bringing about emotional change in our life. And our emotions, as part of the same system, are themselves levers for changing what we think and what we do.

We can change the way we feel by changing the way we think. David Burns, one of the founders of cognitive therapy, writes: "Your emotions follow your thoughts just as surely as baby ducks follow their mothers."[59] For example, one of the main factors that determines whether or not a painful emotion develops into a pathology is how we think about it—as *temporary* and fleeting or as *permanent* and here-to-stay.[60] The difference between sadness and depression is that depression is sadness without hope.

Our deeds, our behaviors, provide another lever through which we can positively impact our emotional wellbeing. While respecting the way we feel is important—giving ourselves the permission to be human—there are times when we can behave ourselves out of an emotional predicament.[61] We feel more courageous the more we act courageously; we become more joyful by expressing joy. As Thich Nhat Hanh wrote: "Sometimes your joy is the source of your smile, but sometimes your smile can be the source of your joy."[62]

The symptomatic approach to our emotional state leads to pessimism; in contrast, the systematic approach to our emotional state breeds optimism. When we look at emotions as static and independent rather than as dynamic and interdependent, the points of leverage remain unseen and untapped. When we don't see connections, we're unlikely to see what led to an emotion and what is likely to lead out of it. In contrast, by identifying interconnections and points of leverage, systems thinking points to the dynamic nature of emotions and hence to the possibility of change. If we feel sad or concerned or angry, we can identify the underlying causes in the form of thoughts and deeds, and then do what is necessary to change them.

*   *   *

The twelve basic principles of Wholebeing are interconnected, each contributing to the whole, and each affected by the whole. The Wholebeing approach represents the cooperative co-existence of interdependent parts, rather than cut-throat competition among independent entities.

This approach is neither trivial nor self-evident. Influential theologies and philosophies—many of the *isms* that have shaped individuals and society—openly call for dismembering parts of the whole and pitting some elements in opposition to others. For example, some approaches treat the physical body as dirty and despicable, while others throw out spirituality as harmful fantasy; some dismiss the intellect, while others treat emotions as detrimental. Then there are those who call for a clear relationship of superior and inferior among the elements. David Hume, for example, believed that "reason is and ought only be a slave to the passions,"[63] while Plato argued for the exact opposite.[64]

The Wholebeing approach calls for harmony among the different elements that make up a human being, and harmony among and within academic disciplines. A beautiful symphony brings together a diversity of notes and chords, of instruments and people, and each part plays an important role, as it contributes its share to the harmonious whole. And so in a beautiful life. Our spiritual, physical, intellectual, relational, and emotional parts can coexist, not as master and slave, but as equals; not with disrespect or scorn, but with mutual respect and reverence; not in discord, but in harmony. This is Wholebeing.

NOTES

1. Rand, A. (1986). Capitalism: *The Unknown Ideal*. Signet.
2. Ibid.
3. James, W. (1982). *The Varieties of Religious Experiences: A Study in Human Nature*. Penguin Classics.
4. Hume, D. (1985). *A Treatise of Human Nature*. Penguin Books.

Moore, G. E. (2012). *Principia Ethica*. Digireads Publishing.

5. Lyubomirsky, S., King, L. and Diener, E. (2005). The Benefits of Frequent Positive Affect: Does Happiness Lead to Success? *Psychological Bulletin, 131,* 803–855.

6. Kristin Layous, K., Nelson, S. K., Kurtz, J. L. and Lyubomirsky, S. (2017). What Triggers Prosocial Effort? A Positive Feedback Loop Between Positive Activities, Kindness, and Well-Being. *The Journal of Positive Psychology, 12,* 385–398.

7. Lyubomirsky, S., Sheldon, K. M. and Schkade, D. (2005). Pursuing happiness: the architecture of sustainable change. *Review of general psychology, 9,* 111.

8. Isen, A. M. and Levin, P. F. (1972). Effect of Feeling Good on Helping: Cookies and Kindness. *Journal of Personality and Social Psychology, 21,* 384–388.

9. Kim, S. and Ferraro, K. S. (2014). Do Productive Activities Reduce Inflammation in Later Life? Multiple Roles, Frequency of Activities, and C-Reactive Protein. *The Gerontologist, 54,* 830–839.

Schreier, H. M. C., Schonert-Reichl, K. A. and Chen, E. (2013). Effect of Volunteering on Risk Factors for Cardiovascular Disease in Adolescents: A Randomized Controlled Trial. *JAMA Pediatrics, 167,* 327–332.

10. Baumeister, R. F., Vohs, K. D., Aaker, J. and Grabinsky, E. N. (2013). Some Differences Between a Happy Life and a Meaningful Life. *Journal of Positive Psychology, 8,* 505–516.

11. Damon, W. (2009). *The Path to Purpose: How Young People Find Their Calling in Life*. Free Press.

12. Wheatley, M. (2002). It's An Interconnected World. *Shambhala Sun*.

13. Damon, W. (2009). *The Path to Purpose: How Young People Find Their Calling in Life*. Free Press.

14. Ratey, J. J. (2013). *Spark: The Revolutionary New Science of Exercise and the Brain*. Little, Brown and Company.

15. Opitz, D. and Melleby, D. (2007). *The Outrageous Idea of Academic Faithfulness: A Guide for Students*. Brazos Press.

16. Spirituality. (1989). *Oxford English Dictionary*. Oxford University Press.

17. Frankl, V. (2006). *Man's Search for Meaning*. Beacon Press.

18. Damon, W. (2009). *The Path to Purpose: How Young People Find Their Calling in Life*. Free Press.

19. Kundtz, D. (2006). *Moments in Between: The Art of the Quiet Mind*. Conari Press.

20. Csikszentmihalyi, M. (1999). If We Are So Rich, Why Aren't We Happy? *American Psychologist, 54,* 821–827.

21. Bennett-Goleman, T. (2002). *Emotional Alchemy: How the Mind Can Heal the Heart*. Harmony.
22. Sreechinth, C. (2018). *Thich Nhat Hanh Quotes*. UB Tech.
23. Descartes, R. (1998). *Discourse on Method*. Hackett Classic.
24. Benson, H. (1997). *Timeless Healing: The Power and Biology of Belief.* Scribner.
25. Cherkin, D. C., et al. (2016). Effect of Mindfulness-Based Stress Reduction vs Cognitive Behavioral Therapy or Usual Care on Back Pain and Functional Limitations in Adults With Chronic Low Back Pain: A Randomized Clinical Trial. *JAMA, 315*, 1240–9.
    Sarno, J. E. (1991). *Healing Back Pain: The Mind-Body Connection*. Warner Books.
26. Ratey, J. J. (2013). *Spark: The Revolutionary New Science of Exercise and the Brain*. Little, Brown and Company.
27. Roger, A. H., et al. (2019). Nutritional Psychiatry: Towards Improving Mental Health by What You Eat. *European Neuropsychopharmacology, 29*, 1321–1332.
28. Field, T. (2003). *Touch*. A Bradford Book.
29. Kabat-Zinn, J. (2013). *Full Catastrophe Living: Using the Wisdom of Your Body and Mind to Face Stress, Pain, and Illness*. Bantam.
30. Bacon, F. (2018). *The New Organon (Novum Organum)*. Lulu Publishing.
31. Ratey, J. J. (2015). *Go Wild: Eat Fat, Run Free, Be Social and Follow Evolution's Other Rules for Total Health and Wellbeing*. Little, Brown and Company.
32. Buettner, D. (2012). *The Blue Zones: 9 Lessons for Living Longer from the People Who've Lived the Longest*. National Geographic.
33. Kashdan, T. B. (2010). *Curiosity: The Missing Ingredient to a Fulfilling Life*. Harper Perennial.
34. Ayres, E. (2016). *Defying Dystopia: Going on with the Human Journey After Technology Fails Us*. Routledge.
35. Carstensen, L. (2011). *A Long Bright Future: Happiness, Health, and Financial Security in an Age of Increased Longevity*. Public Affairs.
36. Aristotle. (1954). *The Nicomachean Ethics* (D. Ross, Trans.). Oxford University Press.
37. Adams, A., Adams, J. and Hogan, M. A. (ed.). 2010. *My Dearest Friend: Letters of Abigail and John Adams*. Belknap Press.
38. Gilbert, D. (2007). *Stumbling on Happiness*. Vintage.
39. Gardner, H. (2006). *Multiple Intelligences: New Horizons*. Basic Books.
40. Russel, B. (2019). *The Conquest of Happiness*. Snowball Publishing.

41. Waldinger, R. (2015). What Makes a Good Life? Lessons From the Longest Study on Happiness. *Ted.com*. https://www.ted.com/talks/robert_waldinger_what_makes_a_good_life_lessons_from_the_longest_study_on_happiness (accessed August 22, 2019).

42. Helliwell, J., Layard, R. and Sachs, J. (2019). World Happiness Report. https://worldhappiness.report/ed/2019/ (accessed August 23, 2019).

43. Bacon, F. (2017). *Essays of Francis Bacon*. Start Publishing.

44. Kasser, T. and Ryan, R. M. (1993). A Dark Side of the American Dream: Correlates of Financial Success as a Central Life Aspiration. *Journal of Personality and Social Psychology, 65*, 410–422.

45. Klinenberg, E. (2013). *Going Solo: The Extraordinary Rise and Surprising Appeal of Living Alone*. Penguin Books.

46. Ibid.

47. Davidson, R. J. and Harrington, A. (2001). *Visions of Compassion: Western Scientists and Tibetan Buddhists Examine Human Nature*. Oxford University Press.

48. Ibid.

49. Ibid.

50. Finney, S. and Sagal, J. T. (2016). *The Way of the Teacher: A Path for Personal Growth and Professional Fulfillment*. Rowman & Littlefield Publishers.

51. Fredrickson, B. L. (2001). The Role of Positive Emotions in Positive Psychology: The Broaden-and-Build Theory of Positive Emotions. *American Psychologist, 56*, 218–226.

52. Brach, T. (2004). *Radical Acceptance: Embracing Your Life with the Heart of a Buddha*. Bantam.
    Brown, B. (2010). *The Gifts of Imperfection: Let Go of Who You Think You're Supposed to Be and Embrace Who You Are*. Hazelden Publishing.

53. Wegner, D. M. (1994). *White Bears and Other Unwanted Thoughts: Suppression, Obsession, and the Psychology of Mental Control*. The Guilford Press.

54. Pennebaker, J. W. (1997). *Opening Up: The Healing Power of Expressing Emotions*. The Guilford Press.

55. Williams, M., et al. (2007). *The Mindful Way Through Depression: Freeing Yourself from Chronic Unhappiness*. The Guilford Press.

56. Spencer, V. E. (2003). *Playing by the Rules: Break the Rules and You're Out of the Game*. Xulon Press.

57. Ben-Shahar, T. (2010). *Being Happy: You Don't Have to Be Perfect to Lead a Richer, Happier Life*. McGraw-Hill Education.

58. Senge, P. M. (2006). *The Fifth Discipline: The Art and Practice of the Learning Organization*. Doubleday.

59. Burns, D. D. (1999). *Feeling Good: The New Mood Therapy*. William Morrow.

60. Seligman, M. E. P. (2006). *Learned Optimism: How to Change Your Mind and Your Life*. Vintage.
61. Wiseman, R. (2013). *The As If Principle: The Radically New Approach to Changing Your Life*. Free Press.
62. Hanh, T. N. (1999). *The Miracle of Mindfulness: An Introduction to the Practice of Meditation* (M. Ho, Trans.). Beacon Press.
63. Hume, D. (1985). *A Treatise of Human Nature*. Penguin Books.
64. Plato (1991). *The Republic* (A. Bloom, Trans.). Basic Books.

CHAPTER 5

Enter the Matrix

I've learned that I still have a lot to learn.
—Maya Angelou[1]

In the previous chapter, I suggested that the twelve principles provide the design for the structure that accommodates the field of happiness studies. My choice to use a building metaphor to capture the role of the principles is purposeful: I'm attempting to create a home for the interdisciplinary field of happiness studies.

To turn a building into a home, however, structure is not enough; the structure needs to be filled with substance, such as furniture, books, appliances, artwork and most importantly people. The substance inside the home of happiness studies includes texts, works of art and people—thinkers and practitioners. With this concept of what the home of happiness studies will look like in terms of structure and substance, we can better imagine the structure and substance of a university course, a certificate or degree program, or a whole school dedicated to life's ultimate currency.

The structure I propose for the field of happiness studies begins from the knowledge that happiness is Wholebeing, and is defined by the twelve principles I articulated in the previous chapter. To fill the structure with substance, we can turn to various existing disciplines for their take on each

© The Author(s), under exclusive license to Springer Nature Switzerland AG 2021
T. Ben-Shahar, *Happiness Studies*,
https://doi.org/10.1007/978-3-030-64869-5_5

of the twelve principles—which is a lot of substance! The many disciplines, from economics to psychology, from philosophy to theology, from art to literature, from history to sociology, from physics to biology, and on and on, all contribute to our understanding of each of the twelve principles.

Combining structure and substance, the home of the field of happiness studies takes the shape of a matrix, with the twelve principles on the horizontal axis and the various disciplines on the vertical axis. Each intersection between a principle and a discipline holds within it a great deal of content in the form of texts or works of art, ideas and practices (see Table 5.1).

While I've merely provided one example within each box of the matrix, there are potentially dozens and even hundreds of works at the intersection of each principle and discipline: writings in different areas, artworks from different eras, and films from Hollywood to Bollywood. The matrix depicted above is also far from complete, in that there are a number of additional disciplines that can and do contribute significantly to the interdisciplinary field of happiness studies: sociology, anthropology, physics and geography, to name a few. The matrix brings together the humanities and the sciences, East and West, ancient wisdom and modern research, all for the purpose of better understanding, pursuing and attaining happiness.

* * *

The variety of relevant substance for the matrix speaks to why the interdisciplinary approach to happiness is universally appealing. Everyone, regardless of cultural or personal taste, can find something to relate to and contribute. Below, I'll elaborate on one example from each of the twelve principles (bolded in the chart above) to provide a sense of the potential breadth and depth of the field of happiness studies. Given the interconnected nature of the five SPIRE elements, many of the works can of course fit into more than one of the boxes.

- The 1938 film *You Can't Take It With You*, which won the Academy Award for Best Picture,[2] contrasts two worldviews. The first, represented by a powerful and ruthless banker, touts money and power as the highest ends; the second, represented by a modest and kind-hearted family, assigns happiness the top spot on the goal hierarchy. The film makes a strong case for the first Wholebeing principle (W1): *The aim of life is and ought to be wholeperson wellbeing.*

Table 5.1 The happiness studies matrix

	Wholebeing		Spiritual		Physical		Intellectual		Relational		Emotional	
	W1	W2	S1	S2	P1	P2	I1	I2	R1	R2	E1	E2
Psychology	Flourish	The Fifth Discipline	Man's Search for Meaning	Full Catastrophe Living	Healing Back Pain	Spark	Creating Minds	**The Absorbent Mind**	Passionate Marriage	**Self-Analysis**	White Bears and Other Unwanted Thoughts	Redirect
Economics	Happiness: A Revolution in Economics	A Wealth of Nations	Conscious Capitalism	Politics of Gross National Happiness	Cost-Effectiveness of Mind-Body Medicine Interventions	A Conflict of Vision	Economic Benefits of Lifelong Learning	Multiple Intelligence in the Economics Classroom	The Economics of Love and Marriage	Self-Esteem and Earnings	Theory of Moral Sentiments	**Thrive**
Philosophy	On Happiness	Everyday Ubuntu	Nicomachean Ethics	Zen Mind, Beginners Mind	Yoga Sutras	The Philosophy of Food	**The Analects**	Philosophy as a Way of Life	**The Subjection of Women**	On Friendship	Tao Te Ching	Meditations
Biology	The Epigenetics Revolution	**Silent Spring**	A Meaningful Life is a Healthy Life	Altered Traits	Descartes Error	Basic Biology of Sleep	The Psychology and Neuroscience of Curiosity	The Neuroscience of Reading	The Neuro-Endocrinology of Social Isolation	The Neurobiology of self-esteem and Aggression	The Emotional Life of Your Brain	The Telomere Effect
History	Heroes of History	Homo Sapiens	The History of the decline and fall of the Roman Empire	Zen Buddhism: A History	The Evolution of Mind-Body Dualism	**The Blue Zones**	Leonardo da Vinci	Life of Alexander	Founding Brothers	The Second Sex	What is the History of Emotions?	Aaron T Beck
Art	Motionless Journey	Garden of Human Delights	The Sistine Chapel	Red Poppy	**The Thinker**	Dancers VIII	Young Man Reading by Candlelight	The School of Athens	Denouement	Vitruvian Man	Chatterton	The CBT Art Activity Book

(*continued*)

Table 5.1 (continued)

	Wholebeing		Spiritual		Physical		Intellectual		Relational		Emotional	
	W1	W2	S1	S2	P1	P2	I1	I2	R1	R2	E1	E2
Film	**You Can't Take It with You**	It's A Wonderful Life	The Matrix	Seven Years in Tibet	Leap of Faith	Wall-E	The Miracle Worker	Idiocracy	Mississippi Masala	We the Living	Remains of the Day	Life is Beautiful
Theology	The Four Noble Truths	Summa Theologica	Bhagavad Gita	**Passage Meditation**	Religion and Spirituality. Linkages to physical health.	Hilchot Deot	Religion for Atheists	Nurturing a Society of Learners	The Story of the Good Samaritan	I and Thou	The Story of Joseph and his brothers	Optimism
Literature	The Eudaimonic Turn	The Blindmen and the Elephant	**Three Hermits**	Siddhartha	The Thinker (poem)	What I talk about when I talk about running	The Chambered Nautilus	The Shepherd of King Admetus	Middlemarch	Things Fall Apart	**On Joy and Sorrow**	Mules and Men

- The 1962 book *Silent Spring* by Rachel Carson[3] essentially launched the environmentalist movement as we know it today. In it, Carson discusses the interconnectedness of all things, and convincingly demonstrates that when humans use pesticides and emit carbon dioxide, they are harming the entire ecosystem and thereby endangering the future of our whole planet. Her book, which falls within the disciplinary realm of biology, makes a compelling case for the second Wholebeing principle (W2): *Everything is interconnected.*
- In his short and brilliant poem "Harlem,"[4] Langston Hughes asks, "What happens to a dream deferred? Does it dry up, like a raisin in the sun?" What happens to a purpose or a calling that is denied us, or that we neglect? Hughes's poem squarely falls at the intersection between literature and the first spiritual principle (S1)—*A purposeful life is a spiritual life.* To lead a spiritual life, suggests Langston, it is not enough to have a dream. We need to live our dream.
- *Passage Meditation,*[5] a book by English professor and spiritual teacher Eknath Easwaran, provides an eight-part program of transformation. The first part is the foundation of the program; it involves silently reading and re-reading a single passage from one of the world's great religious traditions. While Easwaran provides a list of recommended texts, including Psalm 23 and the Prayer of Saint Francis, we are encouraged to pick a text that we intimately connect to and find personally meaningful. In this book Easwaran is urging us to engage mindfully with a theological text for the purpose of enjoying a spiritual experience. This is an expression of the second spiritual principle (S2): *The ordinary is elevated to the extraordinary through mindful presence.*
- Auguste Rodin's bronze sculpture *The Thinker* beautifully represents the connection between mind and body in the form of a man who resides in deep contemplation—in the world of the mind—and yet is anything but detached from the physical world, the world of the body. His body and hand are curled in the shape of a coil. Everything about his posture suggests a physical spiral that is about to unleash its potential energy and erupt, manifesting his thought in the material world. This sculpture is a powerful depiction of the first physical principle (P1): *Mind and body are connected* (see Fig. 5.1).

Fig. 5.1 Auguste Rodin, The Thinker, 1904, bronze. Detroit Institute of Arts, Gift of Horace H. Rackham, 22.143. (Photo courtesy of Danita Delimont/Alamy Stock Photo)

- Dan Buettner's book *The Blue Zones*[6] is an examination of regions in the world where people live the longest as a result of lifestyle choices. People in these regions—from the Japanese Island of Okinawa to the town of Loma Linda, California—are more likely to be in good health and fully functioning well into their nineties and beyond. While the book could comfortably find itself in a number of disciplinary rows in the matrix, I chose history, because *The Blue Zones* describes lifestyle practices and habits that have survived the oft-corrupting crush of modernity. Buettner's book sheds light on the second physical principle (P2): *A healthy life requires adherence to our given nature.*
- The *Analects*,[7] attributed to Confucius, the Chinese philosopher who lived 2500 years ago, contribute in an important way to our understanding of intellectual wellbeing. Confucius highlights the essence of the first intellectual principle (I1)—*Curiosity and openness help us make the most of what life has to offer*—and underscores the importance of an inquisitive mind and an insatiable appetite for experiences, the virtues of lifelong learning and exploration.
- Maria Montessori "revolutionized the system of education in the world."[8] A central idea in her approach to education, elaborated in her book *The Absorbent Mind*,[9] is the child's ability to be absorbed in an activity. When in this state of full engagement, children fulfill their intellectual potential, as their mental capacities and energy levels increase. In other words, they enjoy both peak experience as well as peak performance—both happiness and learning. Walking into a Montessori classroom is often a clear illustration of the second intellectual principle (I2) that *Engaging in deep learning fulfills our potential as rational animals.*
- John Stuart Mill's treatise on *The Subjection of Women*,[10] written in the 1860s in collaboration with his beloved wife Harriet Taylor Mill, describes the potential for happiness that exists in a relationship between equals—an uncommon and rarely condoned idea in the nineteenth century. This single book brought about a revolution in people's expectations of relationships, revealing the hitherto unrealized possibilities for happiness in love—and it also became one of the central pillars of the twentieth-century feminist movement. Mill, the philosopher in love, clearly understood the first relational principle (R1), that *Relationships are crucial for a full and fulfilling life.*

- Karen Horney, born in 1885, was a German psychoanalyst who studied with Sigmund Freud, and eventually parted with his doctrine because, among other things, she believed Freud's focus on the dark side of human nature was excessive. Her work on neurosis was groundbreaking, and her ideas continue to affect the study and practice of therapy today. Horney emphasized the importance of introspection for both personal development and as a path to forming more intimate relationships with others. Her book *Self-Analysis*,[11] in which she argues that by raising our self-awareness we can help ourselves overcome the majority of psychological afflictions, demonstrates the intersection of psychology and the second relational principle (R2): *The foundation of healthy relationships with others is a healthy relationship with oneself.*

- Lebanese poet Khalil Gibran, in "On Joy & Sorrow,"[12] illustrates how literature can inform our understanding of emotional wellbeing. Published in 1923, "On Joy and Sorrow" emphasizes the importance of giving ourselves the permission to be human—of accepting all of our emotions—as an integral part of leading a full and fulfilling life. "The deeper that sorrow carves into your being," writes Gibran, "The more joy you can contain." He provides us with a poetic rendering of the first emotional principle (E1): *All emotions are legitimate, acceptable parts of being human.*

- At the beginning of the twenty-first century, economist and British Member of Parliament Lord Richard Layard wrote *Thrive: How Better Mental Health Care Transforms Lives and Saves Money*.[13] Government policies, Layard argues, can significantly impact a population's emotional wellbeing, by drawing on accessible and teachable techniques from cognitive behavioral therapy. In pointing out the value of investing in mental health, Layard suggests that happiness pays, and makes a macroeconomic argument for the second emotional principle (E2): *Emotions are the outcome of our thoughts and deeds, and inform our thoughts and deeds.*

* * *

I mentioned at the beginning of this chapter that the matrix can provide the blueprint—in the form of structure and substance—for a course on happiness studies, a degree, or even a whole school. But it is not only the matrix as a whole that is useful for generating a blueprint; parts of the matrix can stand on their own as useful constructs.

Each of the rows in the matrix can provide the structure and substance for an entire course. For example, a course on "The Biology of Happiness" can be a part of a happiness studies degree, or of a degree in biology, or a standalone elective. Taking another row, such as film, a teacher can offer a semester or year-long course on "Film and Happiness"—once again, as part of a happiness studies degree, a degree in film, or as an independent course.

Each column too can provide the blueprint for a course. The row associated with the first spiritual principle could form the backbone of an interdisciplinary course, "Purpose and Happiness," that explores meaning through the lens of psychology, philosophy, art and other disciplines. The row belonging to the second spiritual principle could provide the blueprint for an interdisciplinary course on "Mindfulness and Happiness" that includes both the theory and practice of meditation. And taking rows S1 and S2 together can be a course on "Spirituality and Happiness." There are many possibilities.

The field of happiness studies will evolve, of course, as more is studied and discovered, and the substance and structure of the matrix may change over time. New advances in research, or new interpretations of old texts may shed new light on the pursuit of happiness, and either challenge the principles I'm proposing here or add others that are as important. This is my hope, that as the field evolves it engenders discourse and dissent, for the purpose of better descriptions and prescriptions. My prescriptions are inherently limited by what I and we know today. Just as a national constitution may need to be modified through amendments, so the principles I'm proposing may need to be amended. The structure and substance presented here are intended to provide a conversation starter, rather than an ultimate truth.

The purpose of the matrix, of the entire field of happiness studies, is not to establish a dogmatic structure built to weather any and all challenges, but rather to provide a flexible framework for a dynamic and exciting field of exploration. As Maya Angelou points out, we "still have a lot to learn."[14] It is with this humble mindset that happiness studies can fulfill its ultimate purpose, which is to serve any and all people—to help individuals, families, organizations and communities lead healthier, happier and more fulfilling lives.

Notes

1. Angelou, M. (2018). What I Learned [Video]. YouTube. https://www.youtube.com/watch?v=D4kH6f_ga_A (accessed August 29, 2019).
2. Capra, F. (1949). *You Can't Take It With You* [Motion Picture]. United States: Columbia Pictures.
3. Carson, R. (2002). *Silent Spring.* Penguin Books.
4. Hughes, L. and Rampersad, A. (ed.). (1995). *The Collected Poems of Langston Hughes.* Vintage Classics.
5. Easwaran, E. (2016). *Passage Meditation: A Complete Spiritual Practice.* Nilgiri Press.
6. Buettner, D. (2012). *The Blue Zones: 9 Lessons for Living Longer from the People Who've Lived the Longest.* National Geographic.
7. Confucius. (1998). *The Analects* (D. C. Lau, Trans.). Penguin Classics.
8. Kramer, R. (1976). *Maria Montessori: A Biography.* G.P. Putnam's Sons.
9. Montessori, M. (2009). *The Absorbent Mind.* BN Publishing.
10. Mill, J. S. (2018). *The Subjection of Women.* CreateSpace Independent Publishing.
11. Horney, K. (1994). *Self-Analysis.* Norton.
12. Gibran, K. (2019). *The Prophet.* Martino Fine Books.
13. Layard, R. (2015). *Thrive: How Better Mental Health Care Transforms Lives and Saves Money.* Princeton University Press.
14. Angelou, M. (2018). What I Learned [Video]. YouTube. https://www.youtube.com/watch?v=D4kH6f_ga_A (accessed August 29, 2019).

PART II

Applying Happiness Studies

CHAPTER 6

In the Workplace

Happy employees have more engaging and autonomous jobs, they are more satisfied with their jobs, and they show superior performance in the workplace than less happy employees.
—Julia Boehm & Sonja Lyubomirsky[1]

Why should a company be concerned about the happiness of its employees? Why should managers invest in their own and their colleagues' Wholebeing? There are two main reasons. First, because it seems to me, as it does to most people, that if we can contribute to others' happiness, then we ought to do so. If, beyond a paycheck, a company can pay employees in the ultimate currency, why shouldn't it? Second, because happiness is a good investment. There is much evidence suggesting that increasing employees' wellbeing contributes to a company's financial performance.[2] Happiness pays!

We can more fully recognize the material benefits of investing in employees' wellbeing through a better understanding of the oft-misunderstood relationship between success and happiness. Most people believe that success leads to happiness, that doing well leads to being well.

$$Success\,(Cause) \rightarrow Happiness\,(Effect)$$

T. Ben-Shahar, *Happiness Studies*, https://doi.org/10.1007/978-3-030-64869-5_6

This model turns out to be wrong. A substantial body of research on the subject demonstrates that achieving success—no matter its magnitude—does not lead to long-term happiness. Harvard University psychologist Daniel Gilbert,[3] for example, studied assistant professors who were being evaluated for tenure, a guaranteed lifetime position at their university. For most university faculty, tenure is a major life goal, a clear mark of success. Tenure, beyond affording them prestige and possible financial benefits, would also put an end to a stressful struggle—the race to publish (or perish) could finally be over. They would be free to relax and, by and large, do what they love to do. In contrast, not getting tenure would most likely entail continuing the stressful race or altogether giving up on their academic dream.

Gilbert first evaluated the professors' current levels of happiness, and then asked them how happy or unhappy they think they would be once they receive the verdict. Not surprisingly, most of them said that they'd be extremely happy if they got tenure and extremely upset if they did not. Gilbert then asked them how long they believed their happiness or unhappiness would last. Most professors predicted that, given the importance of tenure, the positive or negative feelings would last a very long time.

The reality was quite different. Those who received tenure were of course ecstatic initially (as they had predicted), but they only enjoyed a temporary spike in their levels of happiness (which is not what they predicted). Within a few months they were back where they started—just as happy or as unhappy as they were before receiving tenure. Those who did not receive tenure were initially very upset (as they had predicted), but their unhappiness as a result of their disappointment was short-lived (which is not what they predicted). Soon after receiving the bad news, their happiness level returned to normal.

Other research shows that even winning the lottery only leads to a temporary high.[4] Researchers from Stockholm University and New York University studied 3330 lottery winners,[5] and while essentially all were elated when they won, they did not report any significant long-term improvements in their happiness or overall mental health. Soon after receiving the prize money, the winners were as happy or unhappy as they were before hitting the jackpot.

But while research and most of our personal experiences clearly demonstrate that success does not lead to happiness—that the model so many of us subscribe to is wrong—there is clear evidence suggesting the opposite relationship between the two variables: If you increase your levels of happiness, you increase the likelihood that you will succeed.

$$Success\,(Effect) \leftarrow Happiness\,(Cause)$$

Summarizing decades of research on wellbeing at work, psychology professors Julia Boehm and Sonja Lyubomirsky point to "a persuasive body of evidence supporting the notion that happiness plays a role in workplace success."[6] Happy people are more productive, perform better on assigned tasks, are more effective collaborators and leaders, and are more willing to take on tasks outside their prescribed roles. These are very important findings, turning the cause-and-effect relationship on its head and correcting a pervasive misperception. Success is unlikely to bring about more happiness; it is rather happiness that is likely to bring about more success.

Applying the SPIRE prism, I will now break down the finding that happiness leads to success. Specifically, for each of the five SPIRE elements, I will provide an example of one of the two principles, showing how it relates to success in the workplace. In the next chapter, I will focus on happiness in schools, and provide an example of the other of the two principles for each of the SPIRE elements, showing how it contributes to students' performance.

*   *   *

- Spiritual 1 (S1)

A purposeful life is a spiritual life
The first spiritual principle is particularly relevant to the workplace, as employees who perceive their work as purposeful, as meaningful, are happier and healthier, more productive and more creative.

In a landmark workplace study,[7] psychologists Amy Wrzesniewski and Jane Dutton observed and surveyed a group of hospital janitors. While the scope of their work, what they actually did, was essentially identical—sweeping the floors, changing the bedsheets and cleaning bathrooms—their perception of their work was radically different. Some janitors perceived their work as a *job*—as something they did solely for the paycheck—and described it as boring and meaningless. Other janitors perceived their work as a *career*—with the primary focus on achieving the next promotion or obtaining a wage increase. A third group of janitors perceived the same work as a *calling*, experiencing a sense of meaning and purpose in their day-to-day work. This third group did not see their role as one of merely sweeping, changing and cleaning; instead, they were facilitating the work of the doctors and nurses and contributing to the health and comfort of patients and their families. Not surprisingly, janitors in this third group were overall happier at work, and as a result performed better than their colleagues who experienced their work as a job or a career.

Researchers have found similar patterns among physicians and nurses, hairdressers, engineers, and restaurant employees.[8] Across the different professions, those who experience their work as merely a job, or even as a career, are less fulfilled than colleagues who view what they do as a calling. Wrzesniewski and Dutton highlight the role of choice in employees' experience: "Even in the most restricted and routine jobs, employees can exert some influence on what is the essence of their work."[9]

Research shows that a "job crafting" exercise[10]—in which employees and employers work together to design meaningful and purposeful work—can improve performance, strengthen the bond between employee and organization, and give workers a greater sense of satisfaction and wellbeing.

A first step in this exercise might be a cognitive one—changing the way employees think about their work. For example, have them write, instead of the usual job description—highlighting the technical aspects of their work—a "calling description": highlighting the spiritual aspects of their work that afford meaning and purpose. Asking employees the following questions can be an important first step: What aspects of your work positively impact customers, co-workers, and perhaps the wider world? Is there something about your work, big or small, that is making a difference?

A second step in the "job crafting" exercise could be a behavioral one—changing what employees actually do at work. Is it possible for you to spend more time on activities that are making a difference? Do you have any opportunity to take on responsibility for something that is personally meaningful to you? The change does not need to be radical to impact one's overall experience of work. Small changes, consistently applied, can and do make a big difference.

*   *   *

- Physical 2 (P2)

A healthy life requires adherence to our given nature
A sense of purpose is a human need, often overlooked in the workplace. But other more basic human needs are overlooked as well, particularly in competitive, demanding workplaces. Managers and their employees would benefit enormously by applying the second physical principle and recognizing that they are living organisms fueled by food and rest, and strengthened by exercise.

One of the most significant predictors of a business's success is the engagement of its employees. Research conducted by Gallup demonstrated that companies with the most engaged workforces are 21 percent more profitable than the rest of the pack.[11] At the same time, a staggering 85 percent of employees worldwide were not engaged while at work[12]— they lacked motivation and were less likely to invest in organizational goals.

Towers Watson, a human resources firm, found similar results in that 80 percent of the 90,000 employees they polled reported not being fully engaged in their work.[13] Furthermore, like Gallup, Towers Watson researchers discerned a strong link between engagement and company performance: Companies with high levels of employee engagement saw an average increase of almost 20 percent in operating income, while those with low levels of employee engagement saw decreases of more than 30 percent. Gallup's American Workplace report estimates that employee disengagement costs the United States approximately $500 billion a year.

Evidence suggests one reason for these low levels of engagement in today's workplace is that most employees neglect their natural needs—for rest and recovery, for healthy eating, and for exercise. When it comes to rest and recovery, too many employees today fail to take sufficient down time, occasionally because they choose to, but more often because of workplace demands.[14] In the past, people took breaks from work when nature called, when the sun set, or when fatigue took over no matter what time of day. Today, through artificial means such as the light bulb or so-called energy drinks, we postpone or even eliminate our recovery.[15] Pushing through work endlessly might be feasible in the short term, but in the long term we pay a high price through rising levels of stress, and declining levels of health and engagement.

Beyond contributing significantly to our physical and mental health, recovery—whether in the form of a few deep breaths, a relaxing lunch, or a good night's sleep—boosts our energy levels and ability to focus.

Recovery is a good investment for us and for our organizations. As an example, the RAND corporation estimates that insufficient sleep costs the United States $411 billion a year, or about 2.28 percent of its GDP.[16]

Nutrition, both the quality and the quantity of the food we ingest, matters greatly to workplace effectiveness.[17] Overeating leads to low levels of energy, and more susceptibility to illness; taking in primarily processed and high sugar foods leads to a temporary energy high, followed by an inevitable slump. The lethargy experienced by so many employees as a result of what and how much they eat explains in part why most people, most of the time, are not engaged at work.

Physical exercise has an effect similar to nutrition on levels of engagement.[18] Harvard Medical School psychiatrist John Ratey calls exercise "Miracle-Gro for the brain" and writes about how exercise "optimizes your mindset to improve alertness, attention and motivation."[19] Beyond the importance of exercise, mere movement is crucial. Being deskbound for hours and hours each day does not just hurt our performance at work, it can actually shorten our lives.[20] More and more doctors are referring to "sitting as the new smoking."[21]

Rest, food, movement: basic human needs, so often neglected, at great cost to both workers and the companies that employ them. As Gallup researcher Jim Harter says, "The whole person comes to work, not just the worker."[22] Companies that acknowledge this are measurably more successful—and their people are happier.

*   *   *

- Intellectual 1 (I1)

Curiosity and openness help us make the most of what life has to offer
For individuals and organizations to thrive in today's competitive marketplace, curiosity and openness are absolutely essential[23]—because they provide the foundation for creativity and innovation. In the past, it was sufficient to have a handful of curious and open leaders at the top to drive the growth of the entire organization. But today, with machines taking over the mindless, assembly-line type of work, this is no longer enough. Creativity, innovation, learning, and growing are no longer a luxury of industry's elites, but a necessity for individuals at all levels of the organization.

How can an organization encourage curiosity and openness to experience? First and foremost, by ensuring psychological safety. Researched by Harvard Professor Amy Edmondson, psychological safety[24] is the confidence that members of teams have that they will not be embarrassed or punished if they speak out, ask for assistance or fail in one way or another. When leaders create an environment of psychological safety, team members openly discuss mistakes and learn from them individually and together; employees grow, as does the company. By contrast, a lack of psychological safety extinguishes the spark of curiosity and inhibits openness to experiences. Team members are more likely to hide their mistakes out of fear and shame, which means learning is less likely to take place. The odds that errors will be repeated are significantly higher, and consequently the organization as a whole as well as individual employees pay the price.

In our fast-changing and demanding world of work, an organization that does not nurture the intellectual wellbeing of its employees, that does not create the conditions for curiosity and openness to experience, is compromising on its potential for growth and development, and therefore jeopardizing its future prospects. When Google searched for the "holy grail" of team success—when they evaluated the teams throughout their organization—they found psychological safety to be *the* distinguishing characteristic between their best performing teams and the rest.[25]

To foster psychological safety in their teams, managers must first and foremost lead by example. When managers acknowledge their own fallibility and shortcomings, when they candidly express their own feelings or mistakes, they are encouraging their colleagues to do the same. And by asking questions, managers are of course modeling and hence encouraging—openness and curiosity.

In psychologically safe environments, we often find managers who actively, and genuinely, invite feedback on their own performance. When they receive the feedback, they openly show their appreciation to the messenger, and then decisively act on the feedback. With such managers in place, individual employees are likely to thrive, teams and organizations are bound to flourish.

* * *

- Relational 2 (R2):

The foundation of healthy relationships with others is a healthy relationship with oneself

Wharton professor Adam Grant describes how cultivating a relationship with oneself *and* with others, applies to workplace happiness.[26] Grant distinguishes between three archetypes: givers, takers and matchers. Givers are generous, and kind; they share information and go out of their way to help others. Takers are the opposite; they take what they can from others, use others, and are stingy with their time and advice, closely guarding their assets. Matchers are about quid pro quo, always calculating and evaluating, ensuring they give no more than they receive in return.

Organizations, it turns out, benefit from having givers—employees who are generous with their time and knowledge. Higher rates of giving among employees predict customer satisfaction, productivity, efficiency and profitability. Giving clearly pays when it comes to the success of the group. But what about individual givers? Do they benefit as their organization does? Here results are less clear-cut.

When studying the most and the least successful employees, an interesting pattern emerges. Among the least successful and productive people in an organization, we find a disproportionate number of givers relative to both matchers and takers. It appears that the success of the group comes at the expense of their own. However, research also found that givers are disproportionately represented among the most productive and most successful people in an organization. Givers are the most successful and the least successful. As Grant writes in his Harvard Business Review article, "Generosity appeared to sink some employees to the bottom while propelling others to the top."[27]

What differentiates givers at the top from the ones at the bottom? While all givers share the quality of being generous and kind individuals, the least successful ones allow others (especially takers) to use them. They refrain from saying "no" and do not set healthy limits on when and how they help; they become, in Grant's words, doormats who fail to look out for their own interest as well. By contrast, the successful givers give others, and they give themselves; they help other people and at the same time do not overlook their personal needs and wants. Personal success meets organizational success where self-care and caring for others coincide.

*   *   *

- Emotional 1 (E1)

All emotions are legitimate, acceptable, part of being human
Poor organizational performance can often be traced to a disconnect between the needs of human beings and those of the larger organization. A company suffers when its people are not allowed the freedom to be fully human—and that includes the freedom to appropriately process and express emotions. In the humane organization, ultimate currency (happiness) and hard currency (money) are both important, and managers care about pleasurable and painful emotions as they do about profits and losses.

Psychologists Richard Wenzlaff and Daniel Wegner demonstrated that suppressing emotions negatively impacts work performance, teamwork and physical health.[28] When we reject painful emotions such as anger or envy or anxiety, these emotions only intensify and become more dominant. Managers who legitimize their own and their employees' full spectrum of feelings increase the overall levels of emotional wellbeing in their organization. There's less anxiety, anger, envy and sadness, and more joy, passion, calm and satisfaction.

Christine Pearson, a professor of global leadership at Arizona State University's Thunderbird School of Management, has studied painful emotions in the workplace for much of her career. She writes: "My research with colleagues has shown that discounting or brushing aside negative emotions can cost organizations millions of dollars in lost productivity, disengagement, and dissipated effectiveness."[29] Managers who are tuned in, who listen and legitimize their own and employees' full spectrum of feelings—without getting sucked into or taking sides in personal grievances—can help people deal with these emotions, solve their own problems, and get back to work.

At the same time, leaders need to cultivate pleasurable emotions. Psychologist Barbara Fredrickson has illustrated that pleasant emotions lead to the "broaden and build" phenomenon—to thinking creatively, outside the box, and to developing relationships and skills.[30] These are the very characteristics essential in today's workplace for individual and organizational success.

An extremely effective way of cultivating pleasurable emotions is through the expression of gratitude and appreciation—whether it is for one's work, one's colleagues, or oneself.[31] The word *appreciate* means both to express gratitude and to grow in value. These two meanings are intimately related: *When you appreciate the good, the good appreciates.*

Connecting success and happiness through emotional wellbeing, John Gottman, one of the leading scholars on the topic of emotions, writes: "In the last decade or so, science has discovered a tremendous amount about the role emotions play in our lives. Researchers have found that even more than IQ, your emotional awareness and abilities to handle feelings will determine your success and happiness in all walks of life."[32]

*   *   *

In today's fast-changing world, the Wholebeing approach is critical for personal and organizational flourishing. In 2001, Jim Loehr, a performance psychologist, and journalist Tony Schwartz wrote in the *Harvard Business Review*:

> In a corporate environment that is changing at warp speed, performing consistently at high levels is more difficult and more necessary than ever. Narrow interventions simply aren't sufficient anymore. Companies can't afford to address their employees' cognitive capacities while ignoring their physical, emotional, and spiritual wellbeing... When people feel strong and resilient—physically, mentally, emotionally, and spiritually—they perform better, with more passion, for longer. They win, their families win, and the corporations that employ them win.[33]

Loehr and Schwartz point to the value of focusing on all five SPIRE elements—for the employees, their families and the company. Managers who genuinely care about the Wholebeing of their employees create a win-win environment, likely to lead individuals, teams and organizations along the path of doing good *and* doing well.

NOTES

1. Boehm, J. K. and Lyubomirsky, S. (2008). Does Happiness Promote Career Success? *Journal of Career Assessment*, 16, 101–116.
2. Krekel, C., Ward, G. and De Neve, J. E. (2019). Employee Wellbeing, Productivity, and Firm Performance: Evidence from 1.8 Million Employees. *VOX CEPR Policy Portal.* https://voxeu.org/article/employee-wellbeing-productivity-and-firm-performance (accessed August 30, 2019).
3. Gilbert, D. (2007). *Stumbling on Happiness.* Vintage.
4. Brickman, P., Coates, D. and Bulman, R. J. (1978). Lottery Winners and Accident Victims: Is Happiness Relative? *Journal of Personality and Social Psychology*, 36, 917–927.

5. Erik Lindqvist, E., Östling, R. and Cesarini, D. (2018). Long-run Effects of Lottery Wealth on Psychological Well-being. *NBER Working Paper* No. 24667.

6. Boehm, J. K. and Lyubomirsky, S. (2008). Does Happiness Promote Career Success? *Journal of Career Assessment*, 16, 101–116.
   Walsh, L. C., Boehm, J. K. and Lyubomirsky, S. (2018). Does happiness promote career success? Revisiting the evidence. *Journal of Career Assessment*, 26, 199–219.

7. Wrzesniewski, A. and Dutton, J. E. (2001). Crafting a Job: Employees as Active Crafters of Their Work. *Academy of Management Review 26*, 179–201.

8. Ibid.

9. Ibid.

10. Wrzesniewski, A., Berg, J. M. and Dutton, J. E. (2010). Managing Yourself: Turn the Job You Have into the Job You Want. *Harvard Business Review*.

11. Harter, J. (2018). Employee Engagement on the Rise in the U.S. *Gallup. Com.* https://news.gallup.com/poll/241649/employee-engagement-rise.aspx (accessed August 30, 2019).

12. Harter, J. (2017). Dismal Employee Engagement Is a Sign of Global Mismanagement. *Gallup.com.* https://www.gallup.com/workplace/231668/dismal-employee-engagement-sign-global-mismanagement.aspx (accessed August 30, 2019).

13. Towers Perrin (2008). Towers Perrin Study Finds Significant "Engagement Gap' 'among Global Workforce. Business Wire. https://www.businesswire.com/news/home/20071021005052/en/Towers-Perrin-Study-Finds-Significant-Engagement-Gap (accessed August 30, 2019).

14. Loehr, J. and Schwartz, T. (2005). *The Power of Full Engagement: Managing Energy Not Time Is the Key to High Performance and Personal Renewal*. Free Press.

15. Walker, M. (2018). *Why We Sleep: Unlocking the Power of Sleep and Dreams*. Scribner.

16. Rand Corporation (2016). Lack of Sleep Costing U.S. Economy Up to $411 Billion a Year [Press Release]. https://www.rand.org/news/press/2016/11/30.html#:~:text=According%20to%20researchers%20at%20the,damper%20on%20a%20nation%27 s%20economy. (accessed August 30, 2019).

17. Grimani, A., Aboagye, E. and Kwak, L. (2019). The effectiveness of workplace nutrition and physical activity interventions in improving productivity, work performance and workability: a systematic review. *BMC Public Health 19*, 1676.

18. Ibid.

19. Ratey, J. J. (2013). *Spark: The Revolutionary New Science of Exercise and the Brain*. Little, Brown and Company.
20. van der Ploeg H.P. et al. (2012). Sitting Time and All-Cause Mortality Risk in 222,497 Australian Adults. *Archives of Internal Medicine, 172,* 494–500.
21. Laskowski, E. R. (2018). What Are the Risks of Sitting Too Much? *Mayo Clinic Expert Answers*. https://www.mayoclinic.org/healthy-lifestyle/adult-health/expert-answers/sitting/faq-20058005 (accessed August 30, 2019).
22. Rath, T. and Harter, J. (2012). Unhealthy, Stressed Employees Are Hurting Your Business: How personal well-being directly affects a company's bottom line. *Gallup Business Journal*.
23. Ben-Shahar, T. and Ridgway, A. (2017). *The Joy of Leadership: How Positive Psychology Can Maximize Your Impact (and Make You Happier) in a Challenging World*. Wiley.
24. Edmondson, A. (1999). Psychological Safety and Learning Behavior in Work Teams. *Administrative Science Quarterly 44,* 350.
25. Delizonna, L. (2017). High-Performing Teams Need Psychological Safety. Here's How to Create It. *Harvard Business Review*.
26. Grant, A. (2014). *Give and Take: Why Helping Others Drives Our Success*. Penguin Books.
27. Grant, A. (2013). In the Company of Givers. *Harvard Business Review*.
28. Wenzlaff, R. M. and Wegner, D. M. (2000). Thought suppression. *Annual Review of Psychology, 51,* 59–91.
29. Person, C. M. (2017). Are Negative Emotions Brewing in Your Workplace? *MIT Sloan Management Review*.
30. Fredrickson, B. L. (2001). The Role of Positive Emotions in Positive Psychology: The Broaden-and-Build Theory of Positive Emotions. *American Psychologist,* 56, 218–226.
31. Emmons, R. (2008). *Thanks: How Practicing Gratitude Can Make You Happier*. Mariner Books.
    Amabile, T. and Kramer, S. (2011). *Progress Principle: Using Small Wins to Ignite Joy, Engagement, and Creativity at Work*. Harvard Business Review Press.
32. Gottman, J. M. (1998). *Raising an Emotionally Intelligent Child: The Heart of Parenting*. Simon & Schuster.
33. Loehr, J. and Schwartz, T. (2001). The Making of a Corporate Athlete. *Harvard Business Review*.

CHAPTER 7

In Schools

One test of the correctness of educational procedure is the happiness of the child.
—Maria Montessori[1]

Professor Martin Seligman, founder of the field of Positive Psychology, begins his presentations on education by asking parents the following question: "What would you most want for your children?" Responses usually include things such as happiness, a meaningful life, resilience, confidence, good relationships and health.

Seligman then asks parents a second question: "What do children learn in school?" The responses usually include reading, writing, arithmetic, history, biology, and so on. Invariably, the two lists diverge much more than they converge; there is little overlap, it seems, between what schools teach and what parents want for their children.[2]

While the second list is certainly important—we of course want children to be literate and knowledgeable—why are schools almost entirely ignoring the first list? It would not be fair to hold the schools fully responsible for this predicament; many parents bear a large portion of the blame. While clearly stating that they want their children to be happy, they make it equally clear that the most important product they expect schools to deliver, albeit at the cost of other products, is high grades—so that their

T. Ben-Shahar, *Happiness Studies*, https://doi.org/10.1007/978-3-030-64869-5_7

kids can get into a good college, receive a prestigious job offer and consequently make a lot of money. The focus on excelling on the second list over investment in the first list—prioritizing success as measured by grades over life's ultimate currency—is a systemic flaw, rather than the fault of one of the parties involved.

This systemic flaw—relegating happiness from its status as the highest on the hierarchy of goals—exacts a high price of students and our society. Many of the countries whose students score highest on international standardized tests also have the highest youth suicide rates.[3] South Korean students, for example—three-quarters of whom attend "cram schools" aimed specifically at standardized tests—routinely score highest on the Programme for International Student Assessment (PISA). But South Korea also suffers the highest suicide rate in the world for children aged 10 to 19.[4] In the spring of 2019, 22 students in the Indian state of Telangana died by suicide after learning the results of the state board intermediate examinations.[5] The news was followed by public debates over whether mistakes in exam scoring or generalized despair over poor academic performance were to blame for the suicides—but such a debate really misses the point. For whatever reason, their studies were making the students miserable; of the 25 who attempted suicide, three of the students had *passed* all of their exams. In the United States, where the suicide rate among 10- to 14-year-olds almost tripled between 2007 and 2017, it seems likely that the pressures of school—where students spend most of their days, after all—had at least *something* to do with their despair.[6]

By reinstating SPIRE elements like meaning, health, love of learning, relationships and emotional intelligence to their rightful place on the hierarchy of goals, the school system can significantly improve students' lives—and without necessarily forgoing conventional success in the form of high grades. In other words, school performance, rather than an end in itself, can become a byproduct of the right focus on happiness. After all, we know that given the relationship between success and happiness, if schools pay more attention to the first list, students will do better on the second list. Stanford professor of education Nel Noddings, author of the book *Happiness and Education*, puts it simply: "Children learn best when they're happy."[7] Children, like adults, are more likely to be engaged in their work, think creatively outside the box, and work hard when they are in a positive mindset.

Fifty years ago, the school system could be partially excused for neglecting happiness and its SPIRE elements. We did not have evidence-based techniques to enhance happiness or resilience, and we did not have enough science around health and relationships. That is, however, emphatically not the case today. We know what it takes to boost each of the SPIRE elements—from helping students find purpose[8] in their lives to teaching them how to listen better,[9] from exposing them to research on nutrition[10] and exercise[11] to evidence-based interventions that generate grit[12] and gratitude.[13]

And yet, Noddings laments the fact that in most cases, "happiness and education don't go together."[14] So how can we make happiness and education go together in schools? I will give an example of each of the SPIRE elements in the context of education, focusing within each element on the principle that I did not discuss in the previous chapter on workplace happiness. Needless to say, the application of the five principles I discussed in the previous chapter are relevant to education, and the five applications that I will discuss in this chapter are relevant for the workplace.

* * *

- Spiritual 2 (S2):

The ordinary is elevated to the extraordinary through mindful presence
Columbia University Professor Lisa Miller, whose research revolutionized our understanding of the centrality of spirituality for wellbeing, points out that "Spirituality is the missing piece from the education of the whole child."[15] The second spiritual principle suggests that the void in education can, at least in part, be filled by encouraging more mindfulness practices in schools.

There is a growing amount of research in schools suggesting that regular meditation improves students' cognitive and academic performance, physical health and relationships with others.[16] Students who spend a few minutes a day practicing yoga are better able to self-regulate their emotions and behaviors. Meditation also reduces the occurrence of negative behaviors such as physical and verbal violence, and psychological problems such as depression and anxiety.[17] And, of course, by practicing mindfulness, students and teachers are more likely to experience spiritual wellbeing—seeing the extraordinary in the ordinary, the miraculous in the mundane.

We don't need to introduce radical changes into our education system to derive meaningful benefits from mindfulness. Starting a school day with ten minutes of yoga, or inserting a minute or two of mindful breathing at different points during the day, would hardly be intrusive, and would create a calmer, more focused, and happier classroom. In 2015, Robert W. Coleman Elementary School in Baltimore stopped punishing kids with detention when they misbehaved. Instead, students were sent to a "Mindful Moment Room" to meditate, breathe deeply or strike a yoga pose. Over the next three years the school saw a sharp decrease in disciplinary referrals—and not a single student was suspended for poor behavior.[18] As the Buddha once said: "Though one may conquer a thousand times a thousand men in battle, yet he indeed is the noblest victor who conquers himself."[19]

Practicing mindfulness in schools, or anywhere else for that matter, can be done formally as well as informally. Formal practice might involve sitting down in a quiet space with eyes closed, focusing on something like breathing or a repeated phrase, such as "I am here now." Informal practice is about being present in the moment, whatever we are doing—be it reading or writing, listening or walking. The work of Maria Montessori, the great twentieth-century educator, is essentially about helping the child enter a state of informal mindfulness.[20] She pointed out that, as teachers, "our goal is not so much the imparting of knowledge as the unveiling and developing of spiritual energy."[21] This spiritual energy is unveiled and developed when the child is fully absorbed, mindfully focused and concentrating without distraction.

*   *   *

- Physical 1 (P1)

Mind and body are connected
In Chap. 5, when I introduced the Matrix, I invoked Rodin's *The Thinker* as exemplifying the first physical principle (P1), concerning the mind–body connection. When Rodin first started working on his sculpture, he planned a statue of Dante entirely cloaked in a long, austere robe. Why did Rodin eventually change his mind and choose to portray a muscular nude figure, rather than the philosopher archetype who is deep in thought and whose entire body is covered? Here is what Rodin had to say about his decision to undress the thinker: "Thin ascetic Dante in his straight robe separated from all the rest would have been without meaning. Guided by my first inspiration I conceived another thinker, a naked man, seated on a rock, his fist against his teeth, he dreams. The fertile

thought slowly elaborates itself within his brain. He is no longer a dreamer, he is a creator."[22]

The term "fertile thought" is meaningful. Fertile refers to the ground, where seeds reside, beginning their journey toward the realization—the making real—of their potential above ground, in the outside world. Similarly, the thought is like a seed; the thought can grow and develop and realize its potential outside the mind, in the external world. Yes, Rodin's thinker starts off as a dreamer, contemplating on a rock, thinking. But that is only the beginning, and from a dreamer he becomes a creator. A creator is the person who both dreams and acts, thinks and does, embodying the connection between mind and body.

It's easy to point out where schools are coming up short today in recognizing the body–mind connection. Despite mountains of evidence[23] linking physical activity to better information processing and retrieval, improved attention, better coping and more positive attitudes, physical education programs at schools are being cut. While numerous studies clearly demonstrate a positive association between physical activity and GPA, a 2018 report from the UK-based nonprofit Youth Sports Trust showed that about 38 percent of schools had dropped physical education in favor of greater focus on exams.[24] In the United States, according to the Center for Disease Control and Prevention (CDC), less than 25 percent of kids aged six to seventeen meet the recommended weekly amount of moderate to vigorous activity.[25] Students aren't using their bodies in school. In the words of Erica Lue of the National PTA, "Recess and other physical activities should be viewed as an opportunity to enrich the whole student, and not as a barrier to academic success."[26]

Beyond the obvious benefits of exercise, schools can do more to embrace *The Thinker* as an archetype, a role model, for *The Student*. In a Wholebeing school, learning is guided by the often forgotten principle put forth in the early twentieth century by John Dewey, the North American educational reformer: students learn better by *doing*, rather than by passively receiving information.[27] *The Student*, like *The Thinker*, benefits from combining reflection and action, thinking and doing, contemplation and application.

Dewey believed children were active, inquisitive and eager to explore—and lamented that schools offered too few opportunities for them to show what they could do. Steve Mariotti, the businessman and schoolteacher who founded the National Foundation for Training Entrepreneurs (NFTE), developed a program that allows students to apply what they know about reading, writing and arithmetic to launch a business idea, detail plans and present their strategy to groups.[28] NFTE programs positively impact students' academic performance in school as well as professional success later on in life.[29]

Dewey's learning-by-doing principle can just as easily be applied throughout the academic experience: students have a far better understanding and appreciation of Shakespeare, for example, when they *produce* a play and *act* out scenes, than when they merely absorb his words through passive reading. Biology students, too, could learn more about germination and photosynthesis by venturing beyond the textbook. Rather than figuratively wear Dante's sterile robe, students can roll up their sleeves and get dirty. They can plant seeds in the fertile soil and then watch them break ground and grow toward the sun.

*   *   *

- Intellectual 2 (I2)

Engaging in deep learning fulfills our potential as rational animals
Dewey's vision of students as active explorers also illuminates our educational system's frequent failure to satisfy our natural need for deep learning.[30] Assessment-focused education often forces students to skim over reams of content, learning just a little bit about a lot of things rather than drilling down and learning deeply about important subjects.

The very first class I took in my first year at Harvard, even before the semester officially started, was a speed-reading class. My reading speed increased fivefold, which served me well throughout my undergraduate and graduate school years, as I needed to read hundreds of pages each week. Today, speed-reading helps me keep up with daily NBA news and the ever-changing Middle East situation. But over time, my over-reliance on speed-reading inflicted a serious cost: my ability to dig beneath the surface of texts, my deep-reading muscles, atrophied, and so did my intellectual wellbeing.

There are many great works—of literature, philosophy, art or science—that are deep and profound, and when we skim the surface of them, we miss their beauty and wisdom. When a friend of mine took advanced placement Literature in high school, he and his classmates were given a week to read Tolstoy's *War and Peace*—at more than 1200 pages, the longest of the more than twenty novels assigned that semester. The unspoken assumption was that nobody would really *read* the book; the point was for students to familiarize themselves with it, maybe read the CliffsNotes, so they would recognize references to it on the AP exam. My friend didn't read *War and Peace* until he was in his twenties—and then again in his thirties, and his forties. He returns to the novel every once in a while, he says, because it reveals new things to him, fresh perspectives, as he reaches different stages in his own life. He re-reads slowly, taking his time to reflect on himself and his place in the world. When we take our time to read and reread, to search and research, we learn about ourselves and our environment, enrich each moment as well as our life as a whole.

There are additional costs to prioritizing breadth over depth. I would argue for the existence of a direct link between the surplus of superficial speed-reading and the shortage of healthy, enduring relationships. Close reading fosters our ability to detect nuances, understand complexity and appreciate that which lies beneath the surface—skills that are important for fostering intimate, deep and lasting relationships with other people. Our inability to deeply *know* a text beyond what we can scan in a minute translates into our inability to truly *know* a person—leading to skin-deep relationships and inevitable boredom.

The modern world provides us with a constant feed of novel information—news that updates each minute, TV shows that are produced faster than they can be consumed, fashions that change with every season. We are not required, and in fact not given the opportunity, to explore beyond the superficial and delve into any depth. Why, then, should it surprise us that when it comes to other people, so many of us lack the capacity to cultivate deep relationships that go beyond the superficial?

Schools can, and ought to, provide an antidote to this phenomenon. Studying and becoming intimate with a book like *War and Peace* or a work of art like *The Thinker* can provide great practice for studying and becoming intimate with a real person. If we want our children to grow up and enjoy deep and meaningful relationships, then we'd do well to teach them the skills for it in school—and introduce them to some great works in the process.

* * *

- Relational 1 (R1)

Relationships are crucial for a full and fulfilling life
It would not be an overstatement to claim that the future moral state of our world depends on schools embracing the first relationship principle. Specifically, schools must go back to basics, and provide opportunities for students to interact with one another, face-to-face, really rather than virtually.

I'm emphatically *not* against online interactions, Internet communities, social media or computer-based learning; much of my own learning, and teaching, is done digitally and right now I'm looking at my screen as I type these words. In moderation, screen time can benefit children and adults, however more and more people today are addicted to screens—be it to social media, video games or pornography. When children spend most of their waking hours interacting with technology, the cost is exceedingly high, for happiness and morality.

Perhaps the primary goal of education is to cultivate moral sentiments in children, so that they grow up to be kind, generous, compassionate and caring adults. At the heart of these moral sentiments, lies empathy.

Sara Konrath from the University of Michigan conducted one of the most troubling studies I've ever come across, concluding that "college kids today are about 40 percent lower in empathy than their counterparts of 20 or 30 years ago, as measured by standard tests of this personality trait."[31] Along similar lines, in the United Kingdom, anti-social behavior—the opposite of caring and compassionate behavior—doubled among high school students, as reported by the Nuffield Foundation's Changing Adolescence Program.[32]

Why is empathy declining? Empathy develops in real rather than virtual interaction, when children play together in the sandbox, fighting and then resolving conflicts, crying and then laughing together in real time. And given that children today have fewer of these interactions, it is no surprise that they have less empathy. Teachers and parents the world over are calling for more empathy education, or "character education," or additional classes in value clarification. And while these classes can certainly help, they are not the answer to the declining levels of empathy and its consequent behaviors—including bullying, verbal or physical violence, and other wrongdoings.

Empathy is the language of morality, and the process of learning empathy is similar to the process of learning a language.[33] While it is surely possible to learn a language by taking classes, a class is no substitute for being immersed in a place where the language is spoken. This is especially true of children, whose more malleable brains pick up abilities—whether to speak Vietnamese or to empathize—more readily and easily than adults do.

The equivalent of a language immersion for learning empathy is an environment where people interact with one another face-to-face. No theoretical discussion of empathy in a sterile classroom situation can replace the learning that takes place through real-life interactions, where children observe the impact of their action and directly observe the emotions of another. While effective collaborative learning experiences are among the most difficult for teachers to design, monitor and trouble-shoot, studies of group work activities—or, at the least, of learning activities that require students to interact with each other—suggest they not only improve critical thinking and problem-solving skills, but also offer opportunities to practice and model social interaction.[34]

To develop high levels of empathy—to become fluent in the language of morality—we need to be immersed in real relationships, interacting with real people. This will not happen unless we, starting with our schools, reverse the trend where the virtual replaces the real.

*   *   *

• Emotional 2 (E2)

Emotions are the outcome of our thoughts and deeds, and inform our thoughts and deeds

Students' emotional health is declining, around the world. In 2003, the Adolescent Mental Health Initiative was founded in the UK in response to "a national crisis" in the form of teenage mental illness. The mental health situation continues to deteriorate, as anxiety and depression levels are soaring.[35] We see similar trends throughout our world. Henrietta Fore, UNICEF Executive Director, points to the pervasiveness of this troubling global phenomenon: "Too many children and young people, rich and poor alike, in all four corners of the world, are experiencing mental health conditions. This looming crisis has no borders or boundaries."[36]

Just as students learn to tackle mathematical problems, they have to learn to deal with emotional challenges. One of the reasons educators have provided for focusing on teaching subjects such as history or chemistry, rather than subjects such as "dealing with painful emotions" or "cultivating pleasurable emotions," is that they feel more qualified to teach the former than the latter. Moreover, we have ways to evaluate a students' proficiency in chemistry and in history, whereas measuring emotions is a lot more challenging. Schools, guided by those politicians who determine educational public policy, are interested in that which can be quantified.

Today, however, the argument that emotional health is unteachable or unmeasurable is no longer tenable. Given progress in various fields—from neuroscience to positive psychology—we have valid, evidence-based methods to help individuals lead richer and healthier emotional lives.

Work in cognitive therapy is at the forefront of this research.[37] The ideas that form the foundation of the cognitive approach to therapy were first introduced some 2000 years ago by Stoic philosophers like Zeno, Epictetus, Seneca and Marcus Aurelius. But it was only in the late 1960s and 1970s that cognitive therapy emerged as a treatment of choice for many psychologists and patients, thereby breaking the monopoly in the therapeutic realm of the psychoanalytic and behavioral approaches.

The basic idea of the cognitive therapeutic approach—that thoughts drive emotions—falls squarely within the second emotional principle. Our interpretation or evaluation of a situation affects how we feel; therefore, by changing our interpretation or evaluation we can change our feelings.[38] For example, those who interpret a low grade in math as *permanent* (I will never do well in math) and *pervasive* (I am not a good student) are more pessimistic and more likely to suffer from depression. In contrast, those who interpret the same event as *temporary* (I will do better next time) and *specific* (it was just algebra) are more optimistic and more likely to be resilient.[39]

In study after study, cognitive therapy has been shown to be as effective or more effective than other therapeutic approaches—and often far simpler. In an intervention program designed and led by University of Pennsylvania psychologist Karen Reivich, young teens saw a 50 percent decrease in depression when they were taught a process that helped them distinguish between rational and irrational thoughts.[40] The Preventing Anxiety in Children through Education in Schools (PACES) project, conducted by Oxford University in 2014, administered cognitive behavioral therapy (CBT) for a year to more than 1300 students in 40 different schools. The intervention, which targets both negative thoughts and behaviors, improved children's problem-solving skills as well as helped them to manage their emotions and stress levels.[41]

Teaching this process is no different than teaching something as straightforward as $A + B = B + A$ in a classroom. While both adults and children respond well to cognitive therapy, it is easier for children to master the techniques. And when they do, they become more resilient and ultimately more effective in school and in their lives.

*   *   *

Just as students learn reading, writing and arithmetic, history and biology, they can learn to cultivate the five SPIRE elements. And it is when schools introduce happiness studies as an integral part of the curriculum, that students are more likely to find meaning in school and life, enjoy better physical health, flourish academically, nurture fulfilling relationships, summon resilience in the face of hardship and experience an abundance of joy in the classroom and beyond.

We want our children, as we want ourselves, to enjoy a purposeful and passionate existence, to live fully, love wholly and learn incessantly. We all want a happier and healthier world, a more moral and more compassionate society. It's about time that schools and the entire system of education wake up to this reality and provide what we all truly want and desperately need. As the Polish educator and humanist Yanusz Korczac rightfully pointed out, "If you want to reform the world, first you must reform education."[42]

NOTES

1. Montessori, M. (1914). *Dr. Montessori's Own Handbook*. Frederick A. Stokes Company.
2. Seligman, M. E. P. et al. (2009). Positive Education: Positive Psychology and Classroom Intervention. *Oxford Review Education, 35*, 293–311.
3. Ashman, G. (2017). Stop Going on About Finland [Blog]. Filling the Pail. https://gregashman.wordpress.com/2017/11/13/stop-going-on-about-finland/ (accessed September 3, 2019).
4. Callahan, K. (2015). South Korean Education: What are PISA results really telling us? *The Synapse.* Wang, Y. and Emler, T. E. (2019). Large-Scale Education Tests Often Come with Side Effects. *The Conversation.*
5. Pandey, A. (2019). 19 Students Commit Suicide Within a Week Since Telangana Intermediate Results Were Announced. *India Today.* https://www.indiatoday.in/india/story/19-students-suicide-within-week-telangana-intermediate-results-announced-1509824-2019-04-25 (accessed September 3, 2019).
6. Curtin, S. C. and Heron, M. (2019). Death Rates Due to Suicide and Homicide Among Persons Aged 10–24: United States, 2000–2017. *NCHS.* https://www.cdc.gov/nchs/data/databriefs/db352-h.pdf (accessed December 3, 2019).
7. Nodding, N. (2004). *Happiness and Education.* Cambridge University Press.
8. Damon, W. (2009). *The Path to Purpose: How Young People Find Their Calling in Life.* Free Press.

9. Gulec, S. and Durmus, N. (2015). A Study Aiming to Develop Listening Skills of Elementary second Grade Students. *Procedia: Social and Behavioral Sciences, 191,* 103–109.

10. Bevans, K. B. et al. (2011). Children's Eating Behavior: The Importance of Nutrition Standards for Foods in Schools. *Journal of School Health, 81,* 424–429.

11. Ratey, J. J. (2013). *Spark: The Revolutionary New Science of Exercise and the Brain.* Little, Brown and Company.

12. Duckworth, A. (2016). Grit: *The Power of Passion and Perseverance.* Scribner Book Company.

13. Emmons, R. (2008). *Thanks: How Practicing Gratitude Can Make You Happier.* Mariner Books.

14. Nodding, N. (2004). *Happiness and Education.* Cambridge University Press.

15. Miller, L. (2016). *The Spiritual Child: The New Science on Parenting for Health and Lifelong Thriving.* Picador Paper.

16. Zenner, C., Herrnleben-Kurz, S. and Walach, H. (2014). Mindfulness-based interventions in schools – A systematic review and meta-analysis. *Frontiers in Psychology, 5,* 603.

17. Semple, R. J., Droutman, V. and Reid, B. A. (2017). Mindfulness Goes to School: Things Learned (So Far) From Research and Real-World Experiences. *Psychology in the Schools, 54,* 29–52.

18. Gonzales, A. A. (2019). What Happens When Meditation Replaces School Detention. *Our Children.*

19. The Dhammapada, 8: 103, *Buddhanet.net.* http://www.buddhanet.net/e-learning/buddhism/dp08.htm (accessed September 3, 2019).

20. Montessori, M. (2009). *The Absorbent Mind.* BN Publishing.

21. Montessori, M. (1989). *The Child in the Family.* ABC-CLIO.

22. Elsen, A. E. et al. (2003). *Rodin's Art: The Rodin Collection of Iris & B. Gerald Cantor Center of Visual Arts at Stanford University.* Oxford University Press.

23. Ratey, J. J. (2013). *Spark: The Revolutionary New Science of Exercise and the Brain.* Little, Brown and Company.

24. EB News (2018). PE in secondary schools being cut from the school day. *Education Business.*

25. The Child & Adolescent Health Measurement Initiative (CAHMI). (2016). National Survey of Childrens Health. *Data Resource Center for Child and Adolescent Health.*

26. Lue, E. (2013). Cutting Physical Education and Recess: Troubling Trends and How You Can Help. *National PTA.*

27. Dewey, J. (1997). *Experience and Education.* Free Press.

28. Mariotti, S. (2019). *Goodbye Homeboy: How My Students Drove Me Crazy and Inspired a Movement.* Ben Bella Books.

29. Beary, V. E. (2013). The NFTE Difference: Examining the Impact of Entrepreneurship Education. *NFTE.com*. https://www.nfte.com/wp-content/uploads/2017/06/nfte_difference_final_report_2013.pdf (accessed September 3, 2019).
30. Csikszentmihalyi, M. (2014). *Applications of Flow in Human Development and Education: The Collected Works of Mihaly Csikszentmihalyi*. Springer.
31. Konrath, S. H., O'Brien, E. H. and Hsing, C. (2010). Changes in Dispositional Empathy in American College Students Over Time: A Meta-Analysis. *Personality and Social Psychology Review, 15*, 180–198.
32. Hagell, A. (2012). Social trends and mental health: introducing the main findings. *Nuffield Foundation*.
33. Hoffman, M. L. (2001). *Empathy and Moral Development: Implications for Caring and Justice*. Cambridge University Press.
34. Aronson, E. and Patnoe, S. (1997). *The jigsaw classroom: Building cooperation in the classroom*. Addison Wesley Longman.
35. Bedell, G. (2016). Teenage Mental-Health Crisis: Rates of Depression Have Soared in Past 25 Years. *Independent*.
36. UNICEF (2019). Increase in Child and Adolescent Mental Disorder Spurs New Push for Action by UNICEF and WHO. *UNICEF.org*. https://www.unicef.org/press-releases/increase-child-and-adolescent-mental-disorders-spurs-new-push-action-unicef-and-who (accessed December 5, 2019).
37. Reivich, K. and Shatte, A. (2003). The Resilience Factor: 7 Keys to Finding Your Inner Strength and Overcoming Life's Hurdles. Harmony.
38. Burns, D. D. (1999). *Feeling Good: The New Mood Therapy*. William Morrow.
39. Seligman, M. E. P. (2006). *Learned Optimism: How to Change Your Mind and Your Life*. Vintage.
40. Gillham, J. E. (1995). Prevention of Depressive Symptoms in Schoolchildren: Two Year Followup. *Psychological Science, 6*, 343–352.
41. Stallard, P. (2014). Classroom-based cognitive behaviour therapy (FRIENDS): a cluster randomised controlled trial to Prevent Anxiety in Children through Education in Schools (PACES). *The Lancet: Psychiatry, 3*, 185–192.
42. Korczak. J. (2018). *How to Love a Child: And Other Selected Works*. Vallentine Mitchel.

CHAPTER 8

In Society

"Happiness quite unshared can scarcely be called happiness—it has no taste."
—Charlotte Bronte[1]

There is widespread, and justified, concern about the wellbeing of our society. Emanating from every corner of our global village are voices that, together, describe a Happiness Lost. We hear lamentations of the modern landscape as a *spiritual wasteland*. We are constantly reminded of the *physical decline* of entire populations. We learn about the *intellectual apathy* of our time and all too often see the *death of relationships*. As a result, all around us, and frequently within ourselves, we're witnessing unprecedented pervasiveness of *emotional bankruptcy*.

The 2019 results of the National Science Foundation's General Social Survey revealed that the number of unhappy Americans had increased by more than 50 percent since the 1990s, even as the economy improved.[2] Rates of depression in the United States are over ten times higher today than they were in the middle of the twentieth century. And while the United States continues a steady slide downward in the rankings of the World Happiness Report, these trends aren't confined to America. We're witnessing a pandemic of unhappiness.[3]

© The Author(s), under exclusive license to Springer Nature
Switzerland AG 2021
T. Ben-Shahar, *Happiness Studies*,
https://doi.org/10.1007/978-3-030-64869-5_8

Half a century ago, more than 50 percent of the British population said that they were "very happy"; today, approximately one-third of the population feels the same way. And the trends are continuing in the wrong direction, in almost every place we look.[4] In China, Korea, South Africa and Australia, we see a rapid growth in the number of adults and children who experience anxiety and depression.[5] In its 2019 Global State of Emotions report, after interviewing 151,000 people in 140 countries around the world, Gallup found, for the second year in a row, record highs in rates of sadness, anger and fear.[6]

These trends are particularly surprising given remarkable progress that has come about as a result of the industrial revolution and the overall rise in political freedom. With the rapid economic growth in many countries around the world, we are on average a great deal wealthier. With the collapse of a number of totalitarian and racist regimes, we are freer. With developments in medicine, we live longer. With the growth of the fashion industry and new advances in cosmetics and plastic surgery, we are supposedly prettier. So given that we are wealthier and freer, live longer and are prettier, why are we not happier?

Going back to our discussion in Chap. 2 about the inside-out and outside-in paths to a happier world, it is of course important to deal with poverty. Scarcity impacts happiness levels directly (by causing pain) and indirectly (through poor choices).[7] However, once basic needs are met, additional wealth is unlikely to lead to more happiness, and therefore material prosperity is not the answer to our collective unhappiness. We, as a society, need something else.

Two of the culprits responsible for the regress in wellbeing, despite ubiquitous progress, are the media and technology. The media, for all of its benefits—such as greater access to information and art, increased freedom, and more transparent democracy—has also done a fair bit of harm. The movies, television, computers and smartphones have brought more noise and distraction, more cheap thrills, more violence, more negative role models and more screen time into our lives.

As technology in general, not just as it relates to the media, is making incredible strides forward, societal wellbeing in each of the SPIRE elements is declining. Here are but a few of the negative side effects of technological progress: multitasking is foiling the focus possible through singletasking; the virtual shackles of the screen are limiting movement; superficial browsing is replacing deep learning; cyber relationships are substituting for real ones; and fake feelings are displayed in order to mask real ones that don't quite fit into people's coveted online "brand."

What, if anything, can we do about the declining levels of societal well-being? In a free society it's impossible to eliminate or even significantly limit the byproducts of progress. Nor is it necessarily desirable. As common sense and history teach us, government controls are a slippery slope that can lead a well-intentioned utopian vision into a harsh dystopian reality.

The key that will open the door to a happier future is to compete in the marketplace of ideas, creating healthy and attractive alternatives that can counter the unhealthy and attractive ones that are currently on offer. In the previous two chapters I discussed how we can foster such alternatives in the form of Wholebeing workplaces and schools. In this chapter I will briefly introduce two additional platforms for generating healthy and attractive alternatives: Happier Media and Happier Centers.

*   *   *

Is the media bad? Before answering this question, here is a related question: Is electricity bad? Well, that of course depends. Electricity can be bad if it generates noise or shocks a person. At the same time, electricity can be good if we use it to play beautiful music or power a life-support machine.

The same is true for the media. On the negative side, the media is harmful to our relationships when it depicts unhealthy role models and provides easy access to pornography; it contributes to our overall negativity by exposing us to mindless violence, and it causes incalculable damage to our physical health by encouraging a sedentary lifestyle. At the same time, the media certainly can be, and has been, leveraged for personal and societal good. For instance, television and the Internet play a major role in the education of global citizens, democratizing information, exposing immorality and enabling open debate and the spread of ideas. During the Great Depression of the 1930s in the United States, people went to the movies to temporarily escape their harsh reality, as well as to be inspired and to regain the strength necessary to go on.[8] Ever since Thomas Edison invented the film projector, fictional or real-life heroes from the movies have inspired millions of people around the world to search for and create meaning in their lives.[9]

The media, at least in part, mirrors the culture that produces it. Yet, at the same time, it is more than a passive reflection of cultural values. The media actively shapes the culture by focusing its lens on particular areas, highlighting and appreciating some phenomena while cutting out and dismissing others. Given the power vested in the media, its role can be to bring happiness to life and to lives, by appreciating the good that already exists in our world and thus helping the good appreciate.

Leaders in the media space—be they producers and directors, actors and writers, streaming services and networks—are at a crossroad, and they have to decide in which direction they steer the media wagon. Their choice at this point will determine where we as a society go; it will also determine how history judges them.

In 1888, a French newspaper erroneously published an obituary for the Swedish engineer Alfred Nobel, who, along with his brothers, had invented several explosives, including dynamite. While their initial intent was to use these explosives in mining and building highways and railroads, Alfred and his brothers adapted them to produce armaments that killed thousands of combatants in the Crimean War and other conflicts. The premature obituary was headlined: "The Merchant of Death is Dead." Nobel, taken aback, resolved to leave behind a different legacy, and today the internationally prestigious prizes that bear his name are bestowed for intellectual and spiritual services rendered to humanity, in the categories of physics, chemistry, medicine, literature and peace.[10]

After a life spent chasing material success—inventing explosives made Nobel an inordinate amount of money—he established a recognition program for those in service of the greater good. I propose just such a program for the leaders in the media space. Right now, too many of them are on the wrong side of history, contributing to our culture's decline. They can change sides, as Nobel did, and serve the greater good. How? By shifting their focus toward the cultivation and promotion of spiritual, physical, intellectual, relational and emotional wellbeing.

The challenge of doing so is that, as media experts often point out, education—or even "edutainment" as it is now called—doesn't sell, and in the ratings war, lofty values are no match for wicked baseness. And the media experts are right, *if* we limit our scope to the quick and the easy and shun anything that requires more long-term investment.

The pull that most people experience toward revealed body-parts or fast-paced violence is primal, instinctual and easily triggered. The attraction toward an Emily Dickinson poem or an Artemisia Gentileschi painting takes longer to cultivate and foster. There is an element of the acquired taste in people's attraction to both the profane and the refined, and while the taste curve may be steeper for easy sex and easy violence, the more subtle desire for meaningful relationships and beautiful art can be acquired with a little more time. The initial investment of time and effort is higher in cultivating the finer desires, but the return on that investment is a lot higher too. Cheap pornography is not the path to satisfying sex, and certainly not to passionate and meaningful relationships; shocking violence is unlikely to inspire deep learning or generate enduring pleasant emotions.

The case I'm making for wholesome media content does not reflect a desire to return to prudish Victorian values, nor is it a product of some other archaic or religious moral imperative. Rather, it stems from a deep concern for the psychological and physical health of people the world over, from seeing the direct impact of modern media on society's wellbeing. My case for a more wholesome media is made on the ground that we are nearing bankruptcy in the ultimate currency of happiness, and one of the ways to stop and reverse our descent is to offer an alternative media to the one that currently exists.

* * *

Happier Centers are physical and/or virtual places dedicated to helping people understand, pursue, and attain Wholebeing. They serve forward the abundance of knowledge—both theory and practice—that makes up the field of happiness studies.

Happier Centers are similar in nature to ancient Greek gymnasiums.[11] While today a gym is a place where one would go for physical exercise, thousands of years ago gymnasiums satisfied people's needs in each of the SPIRE elements. For example, there were lecture rooms where one could hear from local as well as traveling scholars; there were quiet enclaves that provided the right environment to meditate or philosophize about the meaning of life; there were open fields and large rooms with special equipment where one could challenge and exercise the body; and there were places to interact and socialize—including baths, commons and paths. These ancient gymnasiums can provide a good starting point from which we can conceive of modern-day Happier Centers.

A Happier Center can transform a neighborhood; a number of Happier Centers can bring about significant positive change in a city or even a country. What would creating a Happier Center entail? First and foremost, capable leadership. At the helm of each center would be a person well-versed in the Wholebeing approach. While those running these centers do not need to be experts in each of the SPIRE elements, they have to have a solid understanding and a deep appreciation of each element, as well as of their interconnectedness.

Today, too many leaders in the realm of happiness, or self-help in general, are heavy on charisma and low on substance. This is not just a problem that is unique to leadership in the self-help space. After all, the most common characteristic typically associated with great leadership is charisma—that rare ability to arouse fervent popular devotion and enthusiasm. It turns out, though, that charisma is overrated—valuable when it comes to gaining followers, but less so when it comes to building effective and enduring organizations.[12] Characteristics such as authenticity, the ability to listen, and a genuine commitment to learning and serving are far more important for bringing about lasting, positive change.[13]

Leaders of Happier Centers will need these latter qualities as living examples of the Wholebeing approach. As Ralph Waldo Emerson wrote back in the nineteenth century, "What you are stands over you the while, and thunders so that I cannot hear what you say to the contrary."[14] This does not mean that these leaders have to be the perfect embodiment of Wholebeing—far from it. What people need is a human role model, not a flawless robot. Modeling fallibility coupled with the ability to learn and grow from mistakes is one of the greatest gifts a parent, manager or any leader can serve forward.

When it comes to the physical space of the center, much can be done with little. Having a large retreat-like space is of course nice—with a track or a field for running, a hall for dancing and yoga classes, a swimming pool, large lecture halls and small seminar rooms, dining facilities that would facilitate lively conversations, and quiet spaces for meditation and reflection. However, small centers can go a long way too in bringing Wholebeing to the community, or in creating a community. Even a single room in a home or a local school that can be used in the evenings and/or weekends can be enough. It can be a place to host small-scale lectures and seminars, group meditation sessions, exercise groups, book clubs and poetry readings, screenings, and so on. A Happier Center can provide evening classes for adults, afterschool activities for children, and events for families over the weekend.

And then there is the amplifying power of technology. Just as electricity and the media can be used for good or ill, so can technology. Using the wonders of technology can help small and large centers thrive. Through the Internet we have access to the best teachers in the world—teachers who can bring us the latest research on romantic love or resilience, and the most profound thinking on Renaissance art or Confucian humanism. A center, regardless of its size, can host live or virtual courses on African folklore or healthy nutrition, mindfulness meditation sessions run by a local teacher or guided by a world-class expert appearing on YouTube, screenings of Frank Capra movies or a local actor reading Shakespeare sonnets, concerts starring Jacqueline du Pré or a live performance by a neighborhood singing group, and classes on improv comedy or life coaching that can blend online and face-to-face training. There is no limit to the wholesome richness that is readily and often freely available today.

With the help of relatively inexpensive technology, Happier Centers can record their activities and then share it with others. Happier centers can form a network through which they can share original material—from filmed lectures to guiding questions for discussion around a movie—as well as links and referrals to other helpful resources. Each Happier Center can create its own micro community of interdependent individuals who learn and love, who search, support and savor together. A network of Happier Centers—in a neighborhood, a city, a country or even the world—can bring about remarkable change on a large scale.

*   *   *

The change that Happier Centers or the Media can bring about toward a happier world will not happen overnight. As I mentioned, in both high culture and low profanity there is an element of attraction that is instinctual, and an element that is acquired. It of course takes longer to cultivate the acquired than it does the instinctual, which is why it takes more time to learn to enjoy poetry than to derive pleasure from pornography. But if we put in the necessary time to acquire a love of literature and music, an appreciation for great movies and ideas, then our investment will yield great dividends in the ultimate currency. Similarly, for most people, it is easier and more directly appealing to surrender to the enticing screen than to take a walk in the park or go to a yoga class. And yet, the physical and psychological price of mindless inactivity is high. If rather than taking the quick and easy path to superficial gratification, we choose to invest in each of the SPIRE elements, we will find more meaning in our lives, enjoy better health, learn and grow continuously, cultivate better and deeper relationships, and lead emotionally rich lives. We will begin our ascent to a higher, happier, more wholesome existence, and thereby contribute to a better world, a better society.

If we begin to introduce the Wholebeing approach in major societal systems such as in business or education, in community centers and the media, we will sooner than later reach a tipping point. According to Malcolm Gladwell, "The tipping point is that magic moment when an idea, trend, or social behavior crosses a threshold, tips, and spreads like wildfire."[15]

Imagine the following: Children who internalize the importance of exercise and healthy eating bringing their habits home and impacting their families; retail stores and manufacturers making products that cater to the changing tastes; organizations helping their employees discover purpose in their lives, and these employees going home and helping their children do the same; the media providing content that further refines people's tastes creating a positive upward spiral; politicians supporting policies that are compatible with the Wholebeing approach. Imagine, one person at a time, one institution at a time, one community at a time, all leading a society-wide happiness revolution.

NOTES

1. Shorter, C.K. (1896). *Charlotte Bronte and Her Circle*. Hodder and Stoughton.
2. Ingraham, C. (2019). Americans are Getting More Miserable, and There's Data to Prove It. *Washington Post*.
3. World Happiness Report (2019). https://worldhappiness.report/ed/2019/ (accessed September 5, 2019).
4. Boyon, N. (2019). New Global Ipsos Study Confirms a Long-Term Decline in the Percentage of Adults Who Consider Themselves Happy. *Ipsos*. https://www.ipsos.com/en/happiness-receding-across-world (accessed September 5, 2019).
5. World Health Organization (2017). Depression and Other Common Mental Disorders Global Health Estimates https://apps.who.int/iris/bitstream/handle/10665/254610/WHO-MSD-MER-2017.2-eng.pdf?sequence=1 (accessed September 5, 2019).
6. Gallup (2019). Global Emotion Report. *Gallup.com*. https://www.gallup.com/analytics/248906/gallup-global-emotions-report-2019.aspx (accessed December 12, 2019).
7. Mullainathan, S. and Shafir, E. (2014). *Scarcity: Why Having Too Little Means So Much*. Picador.

8. Farr, J. (2015). How Movies Got Us Through the Great Depression. *Best Movies by Farr*. https://www.bestmoviesbyfarr.com/articles/movies-from-the-great-depression/2015/06 (accessed September 12, 2019).
9. Cavell, S. (1984). *Pursuits of Happiness: The Hollywood Comedy of Remarriage*. Harvard University Press.
10. Alex, A. (2016). Alfred Nobel Created the Nobel Prize as a False Obituary Declared Him "The Merchant of Death." *The Vintage News*.
11. Cartwright, M. (2016). Gymnasium. *Ancient History Encyclopedia*. https://www.ancient.eu/Gymnasium/ (accessed September 12, 2019).
12. Collins, J. (2001). *Good to Great: Why Some Companies Make the Leap and Others Don't*. Harper Business.
13. Bennis, W. (2009). *On Becoming a Leader*. Basic Books.
14. Emerson, R. W. (1909). *The Works of Ralph Waldo Emerson: Letters and Social Aims*. Fireside Edition.
15. Gladwell, M. (2002). *The Tipping Point: How Little Things Can Make a Big Difference*. Back Bay Books.

CHAPTER 9

Toward a Happiness Revolution

"People have only as much liberty as they have the intelligence to want and the courage to take."
—Emma Goldman[1]

The purpose of the field of happiness studies is to inspire and support a happiness revolution—a large-scale, society-wide shift from *material perception* to *happiness perception.* Material perception is about seeing the material—in the form of wealth and prestige—as the ultimate currency. Happiness perception is about seeing happiness—in the form of the five SPIRE elements—as the ultimate currency. The happiness revolution is about dethroning the material from being the highest on the hierarchy of values, replacing it with happiness—with spiritual, physical, intellectual, relational and emotional wellbeing. The happiness revolution will take place when enough people understand and recognize—as well as live by this understanding and recognition—that the end toward which all other ends lead is wholeperson wellbeing.

A derivative of material perception is that wealth and prosperity afford the solution to most ailments plaguing society. In contrast, the shift toward happiness perception goes hand in hand with the understanding that the answer to our individual and societal needs requires the cultivation of the

© The Author(s), under exclusive license to Springer Nature
Switzerland AG 2021
T. Ben-Shahar, *Happiness Studies*,
https://doi.org/10.1007/978-3-030-64869-5_9

SPIRE elements—be it in our homes, schools and businesses, through technology, Happier Centers as well as governments.

The shift from seeing material abundance as the solution to personal and societal unhappiness toward recognizing the SPIRE elements as the answer is not a trivial one. Old habits die hard—and the habit of seeing the material as the end all was formed over thousands of years of material scarcity and then reinforced by the tangible successes of the industrial revolution.

In the previous chapter I used the word "pandemic" to describe our current state of unhappiness. There is much that we, as a society, can learn from the treatment, or rather mistreatment, of past pandemics. Specifically, today, as we find ourselves in the throes of an unhappiness pandemic, we're making mistakes that echo those we made in our attempts to end the cholera pandemic of the nineteenth century.

Just 200 years ago, one of the most common medical practices was to withdraw blood from a patient to cure illness or disease.[2] Bloodletting, as the practice was known, often involved the use of leeches, parasitic worms that latched onto the patient's skin and fed on blood. Today, we of course know that bloodletting has little or no benefit—in fact it's mostly harmful, since it can weaken patients and introduce infections. And yet throughout the nineteenth century, well into the Industrial Revolution, it was used to treat cholera—not helping and often making things worse.

Between 1831 and 1854, cholera killed tens of thousands of people in England. A physician named John Snow believed the disease was caused by contaminated water supplies, but had a hard time getting any public officials to listen to his theory. After an outbreak in Soho in 1854, Snow was able to map out the cholera cases in such detail that he convinced public officials to remove the handle from a well pump on Broad Street, around which the cases were clustered. The cholera cases almost immediately stopped. Despite this, public officials refused to accept Snow's hypothesis about the link between contaminated water and cholera. "We see no reason to adopt this belief," they wrote. They shrugged off Snow's hypothesis—and his carefully collected evidence—as "suggestions."[3]

At the same time, a number of physicians were arguing that bloodletting, at best, had no effect on cholera patients—but that they could dramatically alter the course of the disease and reduce mortality by administering intravenous fluids. The work of these physicians, too, was ignored. For another three decades, little or nothing was done to prevent cholera outbreaks, and bloodletting continued to be a centerpiece of cholera treatment.[4]

I see eerie parallels to the past in today's unhappiness pandemic. Being victims of material perception, most people see wealth and prosperity as the solution despite all that medical and social scientists (as well as many philosophers and artists) have been repeatedly telling us about human happiness. Just as the medical establishment did 200 years ago, we're ignoring the available evidence: the accumulation of wealth and the mindless march toward "economic growth" amount to a kind of psychic bloodletting. Upholding material prosperity as the highest on our hierarchy of ends, schools in the "developed" world typically focus on preparing students for success (by which they usually mean material success), workplaces mostly house employees working long hours in meaningless jobs, away from their families, all so that they can accumulate more wealth and buy more things. Material perception reigns supreme, wreaking havoc on society's Wholebeing, and nothing short of a revolution can stop our march of folly.

* * *

To better understand the nature of the happiness revolution, it is useful to contrast it with the communist revolution. Karl Marx, intellectual father of the communist movement, was a materialist. The revolution he envisioned was, first and foremost, about changing the physical structure of society.[5] Communists strove toward the redistribution of physical resources and material wealth. They believed, as many still do, that by radically changing the external reality, they could radically—and positively—change people's internal reality. External prosperity—or, if not prosperity, then at least equality—would lead to internal prosperity. The revolution was intended from the *outside-in*.

The happiness revolution, in contrast, is first and foremost from the *inside-out*. Rather than a materialist revolution, it is primarily about a revolution in consciousness, in the way people see the world. According to the Wholebeing approach, human experience is determined more by our internal perception than by external circumstances (barring extreme circumstances, of course, of poverty, physical danger and such). Marx failed miserably because the external means employed to attain his utopian end were immoral—including government-imposed division of labor, forced distribution of wealth, widespread oppression, and the annihilation of individual freedoms. In stark contrast, the happiness revolution is a *moral, peaceful revolution.*

In a world where happiness is the ultimate currency, there are no conflicts over limited resources. The quantity of happiness is not fixed, and an abundance of happiness for one person does not deprive another. The shift from material perception to happiness perception implies a shift from the redistribution of a limited resource to the sharing of an unlimited resource. A commentary in the book *The Teaching of Buddha* captures the essence of the happiness revolution: "Thousands of candles can be lighted from a single candle, and the life of the candle will not be shortened. Happiness never decreases by being shared."[6] The redistribution of wealth is a zero-sum game; the sharing of happiness is a positive-sum game.

*   *   *

What role, if any, does the government have in ushering in the happiness revolution? The notion that government ought to attend to the well-being of citizens began to take hold in eighteenth-century Europe, during an era known as the Age of Enlightenment. One of most eminent American translators of Enlightenment ideals, Thomas Jefferson, stated it clearly on retiring from public life in 1809: "The care of human life and happiness, and not their destruction, is the only legitimate object of good government."[7] It may seem an obvious sentiment today, but it was, for Jefferson and the other Founding Fathers—and for many others who adopted their ideals in other parts of the world—nothing less than revolutionary.

Jefferson had always understood, however, that it wasn't government's role to *provide* happiness to its citizens, but rather to cultivate the conditions in which people could find their way to it. More than thirty years before his retirement speech, long before he'd imagined being President of the United States, Jefferson authored the Declaration of Independence that formally severed the American colonies from oppressive British rule. He chose his words carefully, borrowing a phrase from Enlightenment philosopher John Locke: "We hold these truths to be self-evident, that all men are created equal, that they are endowed by their Creator with certain unalienable Rights, that among these are Life, Liberty and the pursuit of Happiness."[8]

Where happiness is embraced as the ultimate currency, the government's role is to help cultivate the fertile soil where people can flourish.

The government's role is not—and cannot be—to make people happy, but only to put the conditions in place that will allow individuals to pursue the SPIRE elements. What are these conditions? Life and liberty. First, the government must do its utmost to ensure that each life is protected, that each person is safe from harm. Second, the government's role is to ensure the freedom of its citizens, to safeguard individual liberty. People living in free, democratic countries are significantly happier than people living under oppressive, totalitarian regimes.[9]

Another important role for the government is shifting the population's focus to what truly matters—namely happiness. One of the ways of doing it is by measuring happiness—specifically the five SPIRE elements—in addition to the traditional economic measures. Right now, most governments in the world gauge Gross Domestic Product (GDP) or Gross National Product (GNP), and they have educated the majority of the population to use these measures to assess how well or poorly their country is doing.

In his 2010 commencement address to graduates of the University of South Carolina, Ben Bernanke, former Chair of the US Federal Reserve System, suggested that we look beyond material wealth: "Notwithstanding that income contributes to well-being, the economics of happiness is also a useful antidote to the tendency of economists to focus exclusively on material determinants of social welfare, such as the GDP. GDP is not itself the final objective of policy."[10] Martin Seligman, in his book *Flourish,* also assails GDP as the measure of prosperity:

> What is all our wealth for, anyway? Surely it is not, as most economists advocate, just to produce more wealth. Gross domestic product (GDP) was, during the industrial revolution, a decent first approximation to how well a nation was doing. Now, however, every time we build a prison, every time there is a divorce, a motor accident, or a suicide, the GDP—just a measure of how many goods and services are used—goes up. The aim of wealth should not be to blindly produce a higher GDP but to produce more well-being.[11]

The Himalayan Kingdom of Bhutan was the first country to introduce a new measure of wellbeing: Gross National Happiness.[12] New Zealand, under the leadership of Prime Minister Jacinda Ardern, has recently introduced a "well-being budget" where the focus, in the words of Finance Minister Grant Robertson, is "about making New Zealand both a great place to make a living, and a great place to make a life."[13]

I most certainly do not recommend that countries do away with measuring GDP or GNP. Creating material prosperity and eradicating poverty are two sides of the same coin, a coin that is very much part of the ultimate currency. What I do recommend is that governments additionally measure Wholebeing and its five SPIRE elements.

The promise of the field of happiness studies is to support a world-wide happiness revolution. This revolution can liberate billions of people from the shackles of material perception, and guide them toward a place where they can find more meaning and enjoy better health, where learning and loving freely flow, where sadness and joy peacefully coexist.

Notes

1. Goldman, E. (1914). *The Social Significance of the Modern Drama*. Richard G. Badger.
2. Cohen, J. (2018). A Brief History of Bloodletting. History Stories. https://www.history.com/news/a-brief-history-of-bloodletting#:~:text=Considered%20one%20of%20medicine%27s%20oldest,overabundance%20of%20blood%2C%20or%20plethora. (accessed September 12, 2019).
3. Heinzen, T. E. and Goodfriend, W. (2018). *Case Studies in Social Psychology: Critical Thinking and Application*. Sage Publications.
4. Vigiliani, M. Heaton, G. and Hoose, P. (2017). *A History of Medicine in 50 Discoveries*. Tilbury House Publishers.
5. Marx, K. and Engels, F. (2002). *The Communist Manifesto*. Penguin Classics.
6. Bukkyo Dendo Kyokai (1989). *The Teaching of Buddha*. Kosaido Printing Co.
7. Jefferson, T. Thomas Jefferson to the Republicans of Washington County, Maryland, 31 March 1809 [Letter]. *Founders Online*. https://founders.archives.gov/documents/Jefferson/03-01-02-0088 (accessed September 12, 2019).
8. Jefferson, T. (2019). Declaration of Independence. *America's Founding Documents*. https://www.archives.gov/founding-docs/declaration-transcript (accessed September 12, 2019).
9. World Happiness Report (2019). https://worldhappiness.report/ed/2019/ (accessed September 12, 2019).
   Ott, J. C. (2015). Government and Happiness in 130 Countries: Good Governance Fosters Higher Level and More Equality of Happiness. *Social Indicators Research, 102*, 3–22.

10. Bernanke, B. (2010). The Economics of Happiness. *The University of South Carolina Commencement Ceremony*. https://www.federalreserve.gov/newsevents/speech/bernanke20100508a.htm (accessed September 16, 2019).
11. Seligman, M. E. P. (2012). *Flourish: A Visionary New Understanding of Happiness and Well-Being*. Atria Books.
12. Center for Bhutan Studies & GNH. https://www.grossnationalhappiness.com/ (accessed September 16, 2019).
13. Charlton, E. (2019). New Zealand has Unveiled Its First 'Well-Being'Budget. *World Economic Forum*. https://www.weforum.org/agenda/2019/05/new-zealand-is-publishing-its-first-well-being-budget/ (accessed September 16, 2019).

Epilogue

"Hope" is the thing with feathers—
That perches in the soul—
And sings the tune without the words—
And never stops—at all—
—Emily Dickinson[1]

July 2019. A transpacific flight somewhere between Los Angeles and Singapore. The monotonous hum of the plane, the slow-moving clouds, the intimation of a rainbow that seems within reach stimulate within me a state of gratitude and hope. It's been four years, almost to the day, since I first lamented the conspicuous absence of an interdisciplinary field of happiness studies. Today, it seems to me, more and more seeds are taking root and breaking ground in the field of happiness studies. Thousands of students are participating in the Certificate in Happiness Studies,[2] learning about Wholebeing, SPIRE and life's ultimate currency. A number of universities are currently designing the blueprint for an interdisciplinary degree course in happiness studies. I hear of more and more initiatives in schools, organizations and communities suggesting the imminence of a happiness revolution.

There's much to be happy about. There's much more to do.

NOTE

1. Dickinson, E. and Johnson, T. H. (ed.). (1976). *The Complete Poems of Emily Dickinson*. Back Bay Books.
2. The Happiness Studies Academy. www.happinessstudies.academy (accessed September 12, 2019).

APPENDIX

A few months after completing this manuscript, the COVID-19 pandemic broke out, and then a few months later, worldwide protests over racism and discrimination erupted. For many people, those colossal events tested the entire idea of happiness studies. Sometimes implicitly, more often explicitly, I'm asked the following questions: Shouldn't happiness take a back seat for a while? Shouldn't it lock itself up, quarantine itself in isolation, until the COVID-19 threat subsides, and until protests bring forth real structural change? What is the relevance of happiness when people are concerned about the brutality of a virus that does not discriminate and a sector of society that does?

The short answer is that happiness studies matters regardless of external circumstances. It matters when things are going well, when sailing is relatively smooth; it matters even more in challenging times, when "the winds of change are blowing wild and free"[1] and we're called to navigate choppy waters. To understand why, it is important to understand the idea, and the possibility, of posttraumatic growth.[2]

When I ask students in my class on Happiness whether they've heard of PTSD, most if not all hands go right up. When I then ask them whether they've heard of PTG, rarely is a hand raised. PTSD is, of course, posttraumatic stress disorder—a detrimental and enduring response to a harsh experience.[3] PTG stands for posttraumatic growth—a beneficial and enduring response to a harsh experience.[4] A myriad of situations can

© The Author(s), under exclusive license to Springer Nature
Switzerland AG 2021
T. Ben-Shahar, *Happiness Studies*,
https://doi.org/10.1007/978-3-030-64869-5

generate the trauma—from exposure to war and terrorism to being a victim of a crime or a natural disaster—and every traumatic experience can lead toward a disorder or toward growth.

A pandemic is a traumatic experience on a global scale. The police brutality that led to the protests and some of the subsequent violence can certainly be experienced as traumatic. The question that many of us are asking, whether as mental health professionals or concerned individuals, is what will happen the day after. How will these traumatic experiences affect us in the long term? The short answer is that it could go either way—it can put us down or raise us up, leave us weaker or make us stronger.

The fact that so few people know about PTG, about the science of emerging stronger from a trauma, is troubling. Knowing that PTG is a real option, and understanding some of the science behind it, can produce a ray of hope in an otherwise dark reality. And hope matters. As I discussed under the second emotional principle, the difference between sadness and depression is that depression is sadness without hope.

Furthermore, rather than being passive victims at the mercy of a trauma, we can play an active role in how the experience plays out. And this is where happiness studies can help, as it turns out that each one of the SPIRE elements contributes to growth, in general and particularly following a trauma.

The ability to give meaning to a traumatic event can go a long way in helping us emerge stronger from it (spiritual wellbeing).[5] Cultivating physical toughness through exercise, for example, contributes significantly to mental toughness and our ability to handle hardship (physical wellbeing).[6] Understanding what one is going through and generating a sense of coherence is critical for healing and moving forward (intellectual wellbeing).[7] Reaching out for support to those we care about and who care about us can make all the difference between falling down and rising, as individuals and as a society (relational wellbeing).

When it comes to emotional wellbeing, there are a number of benefits that we can derive in the midst of, or after, trauma. First, when we allow painful emotions to flow freely, these emotions do not overstay their welcome and do not exceed their usefulness. Giving ourselves the permission to be human enhances the likelihood that we find healthy and productive channels for the expression of sadness or disappointment, fear or anger.[8]

Pleasurable emotions also play an important role in the midst of difficult times. A brief experience of gratitude and hope, or a stolen moment of awe and inspiration—even, or especially, when the landscape is grim—can go a long way in helping us come up with creative solutions to personal and societal impasses, as well as provide us the energy needed to overcome seemingly insurmountable obstacles.[9]

In bad times and good times, in peril and prosperity, happiness is a worthy end!

NOTES

1. Dylan, B. (1997). Make You Feel My Love [Recorded by B. Dylan]. On *Time Out of Mind*. Columbia Records.
2. Calhoun, L. G. and Tedeschi, R. G. (eds.). (2006). *Handbook of Posttraumatic Growth: Research and Practice*. Routledge.
3. Schiraldi, G. R. (2016). *The Post-Traumatic Stress Disorder Sourcebook: A Guide to Healing, Recovery, and Growth*. McGraw-Hill Education.
4. Schwartz, A. (2020). *The Post-Traumatic Growth Guidebook: Practical Mind-Body Tools to Heal Trauma, Foster Resilience and Awaken Your Potential*. PESI Publishing & Media.
5. Calhoun, L. G. and Tedeschi, R. G. (eds.). (2006). *Handbook of Posttraumatic Growth: Research and Practice*. Routledge.
6. Dienstbier, R. A. and Zillig, L. M. P. (2002). Toughness. In C. R. Snyder and S. J. Lopez (Eds.), *Handbook of Positive Psychology* (pp. 515–527). Oxford University Press.
7. Antonovsky, A. (1979). *Health, Stress and Coping*. Jossey-Bass.
8. Ben-Shahar, T. (2010). *Being Happy: You Don't Have to Be Perfect to Lead a Richer, Happier Life*. McGraw-Hill Education.
9. Fredrickson, B. L. (2001). The Role of Positive Emotions in Positive Psychology: The Broaden-and-Build Theory of Positive Emotions. *American Psychologist*, 56, 218–226.

Index[1]

---

[1] Note: Page numbers followed by 'n' refer to notes.

© The Author(s), under exclusive license to Springer Nature
Switzerland AG 2021
T. Ben-Shahar, *Happiness Studies*,
https://doi.org/10.1007/978-3-030-64869-5

Printed in the United States
by Baker & Taylor Publisher Services